Rousay Rem

The Endearing Island Childhood of Phebe Marwick

Tom Lennie

Published by intrepid books

Printed in the UK by Cloc Book Print, London.

ISBN: 978-1-9998629-1-6

Front cover – *Innister from Knock'ha* by Mary Arneil

Further copies of this book can be obtained by contacting the author at blueyonder04@gmail.com

This book is dedicated
to the loving memory of
Lorraine Marwick Lennie,
who passed away
January 1964,
aged four.

Mary Arneil – Illustrator/Artist

Mary, aged 90, in her beautiful Brightons garden

All the illustrations in this book – over 130 in total – along with the painting featured on the cover – were drawn or painted by Mary Arneil, a retired art teacher from Brightons, near Falkirk. Like the subject of this book, Mary is also a nonagenarian, having been born less than two weeks after Phebe, on 10th April 1927.

After leaving school, Mary entered the *Edinburgh College of Art* in 1946, where she studied for five years. She taught art at *James Clark Junior Secondary School* in central Edinburgh for two years, before moving to *Portobello High School* in 1954. After seventeen years in this position, Mary was appointed Head of Art at a prestigious independent girls' school in Edinburgh in 1970, a post she held for twenty years. Formally retiring in 1990, Mary continued to teach in various capacities over subsequent years.

Aged ninety, Mary still tutors an Art Group based in Brightons. She lives alone - maintaining as much independence as possible - in the nearby family home.

Contents   Page

Foreword / Endorsement

"Rousay Remembered" is a fascinating and charming slice of Orcadian social history, and it's also a cracking good read. I've just finished reading the book – and absolutely loved it! Phebe's reminiscences have been lovingly recorded by her son, Tom, and provide a series of vivid snapshots of life in Rousay more than eighty years ago. I could taste the clapshot and smell the pancakes cooking on the yetlin - terrific stuff!!

Dave Gray (Senior Producer, BBC Radio Orkney).

Introduction

Every now and then, through the years, an event in the ordinary course of daily life would trigger off a memory in my mother's mind, and prompt her to tell a particular story from her childhood days in Rousay. I always noted how she recalled childhood events in such detail. She could often remember exactly where a brother or sister was standing when a memorable event occurred, even what they were wearing, the very words they uttered, and so on. And again and again, on retelling a story, she would conclude by saying, as if reliving the event, *'I mind it as weel as can be!'* (a phrase used so often that it was actually considered as a title for this book).

These stories seemed rooted in an age so vastly distant to the present day – a way of life so utterly different from anything anybody would be familiar with today. Aware that while then in her 80s, her memory was still very sharp, I belatedly attempted to make a record of my mother's childhood stories. Only to discover that she had little appetite for sitting down and retelling story after story. She preferred sharing these anecdotes in a natural, spontaneous manner – as and when current events sparked them off in her mind. And she couldn't for the life of her see how anything that happened in her past would be of interest to anyone outside her immediate family.

It took a while, but eventually she came round to sharing, one more time, incidents from her childhood – now some eight decades in the past. I have sought to record them as carefully as possible, and group them together under related themes.

Some of the stories are innocuous anecdotes, related primarily for their nostalgic value. Others hold emotional merit, sticking in my mother's mind all these years mainly due to the sense of affection, fun or sadness attached to them. But it is hoped that the main worth of these reminiscences is that, collectively, they offer rare insight into both the day-to-day life on a medium-sized Orkney farm in the 1930s and 40s, as well as the wider social conditions on an island community in these pre-war years as well as during the war-period itself.

Events are shared just as my mother remembers them. While effort has been made to ensure the truth of stories where possible, there is no claim to one hundred percent accuracy. A great many stories relate to immediate family members or to neighbours living in and around Wasbister. My mother was particularly fond of her brothers and sisters and has remained so all her life. All stories referring to siblings and to anyone else living on Rousay during her childhood are shared in very good faith and with every effort and desire to avoid the slightest causation of offence or embarrassment.

I'd like to offer my huge appreciation to Mary Arneil for providing all of the illustrations and the cover painting for this book. With a winsome character and an artistic gifting that is truly formidable, her input to this work has been invaluable. A very special thanks to Sue Begg, my friend and Mary's cousin, for taking on her inimitable role as facilitator. I'm most appreciative of the support of Angela

Thomson, who helped in a beautiful way to make the dream become a reality. And a great big 'thank you' to Margaret Kirkness, who took the time to carefully proof-read the text, also providing helpful advice and encouragement.

Sincere thanks are due to Tommy Gibson, *Brinola*, Rousay, for allowing me to reproduce several rare black & white photographs from his extensive collection. This includes a group photo that my mother had never previously seen featuring her father (she had only ever known of one photo of him). Finally, my grateful thanks to Max Fletcher, *Deithe*, Rousay, for allowing me to use *'Rousay Remembered'* as the title of this book. *'Rousay Remembered'* is of course the name of Max's website, one that offers an abundance of rich information on all aspects of Rousay history, recent and more distant. The entire website is awash with scores of impressive photographs, and the reader is warmly encouraged to peruse its many informative pages.

Tom Lennie
November 2017

Orkney

North Ronaldsay

Papa Westray

Westray

Calf of
Eday

Sanday

Faray

Rousay

Eynhallow

Eday

Egilsay

Papa Stronsay

Green Holm

Linga Holm

Wyre

Stronsay

Gairsay

Shapinsay

Mainland

Auskerry

Stromness

Kirkwall

North Sea

Graemsay

Orphir

Scapa Flow

Copinsay

Cava

Glimps Holm

Lamb Holm

Hoy

Hunda

Fara

Flotta

Burray

Switha

South Ronaldsay

Pentland Firth

Swona

Dunnet Head

ROUSAY

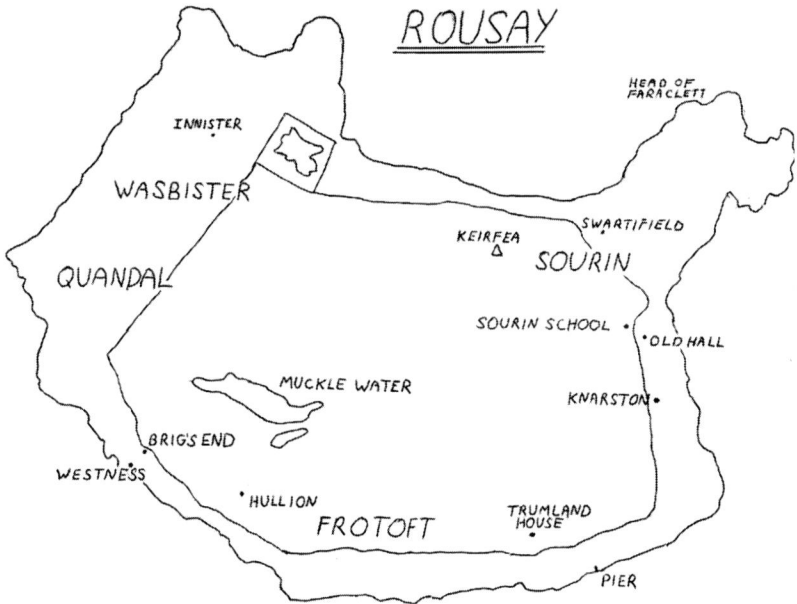

HEAD OF FARACLETT

INNISTER

WASBISTER

QUANDAL

KEIRFEA △   SOURIN

SWARTIFIELD

SOURIN SCHOOL   •OLD HALL

MUCKLE WATER

KNARSTON •

BRIG'S END

WESTNESS

•HULLION   FROTOFT

TRUMLAND HOUSE

PIER

WASBISTER

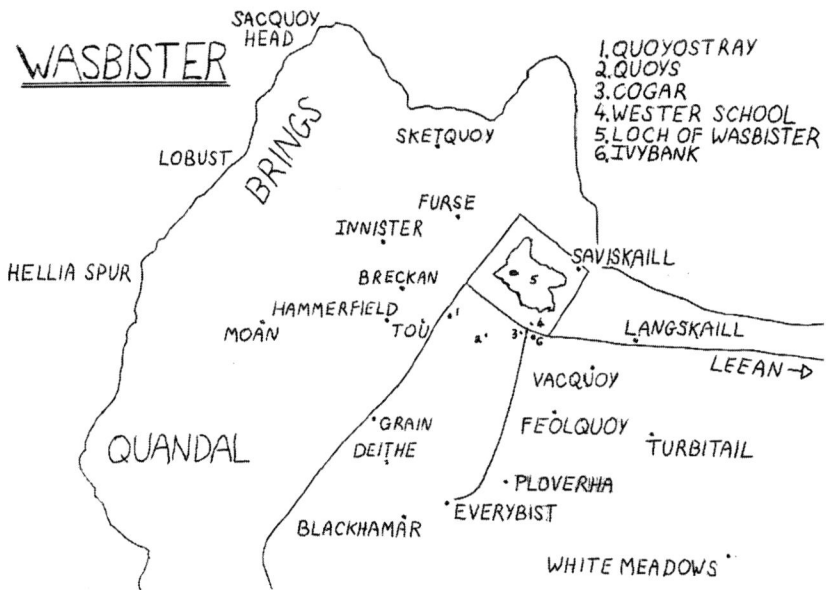

SACQUOY HEAD

BRINGS

1. QUOYOSTRAY
2. QUOYS
3. COGAR
4. WESTER SCHOOL
5. LOCH OF WASBISTER
6. IVYBANK

SKETQUOY

LOBUST

FURSE

INNISTER

HELLIA SPUR

BRECKAN

SAVISKAILL

HAMMERFIELD

MOAN   TOÙ

LANGSKAILL

LEEAN →

VACQUOY

QUANDAL

•GRAIN
DEITHE

FEOLQUOY

•TURBITAIL

•PLOVERHA

•EVERYBIST

BLACKHAMAR

WHITE MEADOWS •

9

Rousay

Rousay is the third largest of Orkney's north isles (after Westray and Sanday). Oval-shaped, it is Orkney's hilliest island after Hoy, being dominated by several hills rising to over 750 feet. Most of the island's arable land is to be found within a few hundred yards of the coastline. One main road, fourteen miles in length, circulates the island, the only Orkney island with a road running round it.

There are six districts in Rousay – in a clockwise direction: Brinian, Frotoft, Westside, Quandal, Wasbister and Sourin. The island's population was close to a thousand in the mid-1800s, but it dropped significantly from that time as more and more people left Rousay to find work elsewhere. The figure stood at around five hundred in the late 1920s. [1]

Rousay is amok with archaeological sites, only a small portion of which have been excavated and researched. So rich is it in sites of antiquity that it has won the title, '*Egypt of the North*'. Influences of Neolithic, Stone & Bronze Age, Pictish and Viking habitation make it among the richest spectrums of settlement to be found anywhere in Northern Europe. The *Westness* area in particular has been hailed as the '*most important archaeological mile in Scotland*', a veritable stroll through five thousand years of history, right up to the mid-nineteenth century clearances.

---

[1] The period during which I was born. The population continued to decrease over the years, dropping to less than 350 by the time I left the island in 1948.

Excavation into Rousay's archaeological history seriously began during the early 1930s, after Walter Grant, one of the Grant family of Grant's whisky, and owner of Highland Park distillery, moved to Rousay. He bought *Trumland House* and estate in the Brinian district as a summer residence, and invited some leading archaeologists to come and supervise the excavation of the island's ancient sites.

The bulk of the ground-work was carried out by Grant's right-hand man, my uncle James Yorston (married to my aunt Bella), accompanied by his teenage son, my cousin Jim. Over a period of five consecutive summers and several winter months, the majority of the cleaning out of *Midhowe Broch & Cairn*, on Rousay's west-side, was performed by the back-breaking labours of this father-and-son team (along with a number of seasonal helpers, who, sadly, have received next to no credit for their efforts). Remarkably, it was estimated that in all, from 1,500 to 2,000 tons of fallen stones and debris were removed in that time – an outstanding achievement, especially given that all the work was done using very basic tools, such as shovel and pick.

Overlooking Eynhallow Sound, *Midhowe Cairn* constitutes Orkney's largest chambered cairn, while nearby *Midhowe Broch* consists of a range of Iron-age fortified dwellings. These sister sites constitute Rousay's most popular tourist attractions by a long shot. Both James Yorston senior & junior were later elected Fellows of the Society of Antiquaries of Scotland, a sign of just how much their excavational labours on the island were appreciated.

Most of this, of course, had little bearing on my early years – I had no idea what all the fuss regarding dirty old stones was about! But I do remember that my older brother, Sydney worked for a spell at the excavation of *Midhowe Cairn* when he came back to Rousay on holiday in the early 1930s.

Well do I mind, also Walter Grant himself. He was one of the very few folk on the island to own a car in the pre-war years – a big posh shiny black one - and his chauffeur used to drive him over to the area I lived in almost on a daily basis during the summer to go fishing at the *Loch o'Wasbister*. We would see them pass through a gate next to the playground of our school, and across the field to the shore of the loch. Here Grant kept a wee boat, in which he would sail out into the loch and fish for trout.

Innister

I was born and raised on the farm of *Innister* (the original name of which, *Ingisgarth*, dates back to at least the early 1600s). Situated in the Wasbister district of Rousay (locally known as Wester), it was a comparatively large farm, comprising sixty-four acres of arable land along with one hundred and forty acres of pasture-land. The modern two-storey house at *Innister* was built around ten years before I was born. You entered via a porch, leading to a large kitchen, which also served as the main room of the house.

Here the Marwicks cooked, baked, ate their meals, and relaxed around the stove fire in the evenings when all the work was done. On colder winter nights we would move to the cosier ben-room to sit. This contained a box-bed and normally served as my mother's bedroom. There were three further bedrooms downstairs - two of them very small. Upstairs consisted of two large bedrooms and one peedie one. *Innister* had no toilet.

Another door off the porch led to the dairy, where the milk was separated, the butter was kirned, etc. The dairy had a slabbed shelf half-way around it, on which we stored foodstuffs we wanted to keep cool, such as blocks of butter, pickled eggs and big jars of cream.

Farm Layout

The *'auld hoose'*, located up the brae at the back of the new house, was where several of my older siblings were born. It consisted of one long building made up of the original dwelling-house, along with out-houses at each end.

Near to the new house of *Innister*, the farm buildings were built in an upturned U shape. The stable was nearest the house. Going along from one end of the stable ran the two byres, and then coming down from the other end of the byres, parallel to the stable, was the barn. Above the barn was located the granary.

Most of the fields of *Innister* were not named specifically, though there were one or two exceptions. Eg, the fields of *Hammer* and *Gorn* took their names from the dwellings that used to be situated at either side of *Innister*, these having been incorporated into the farm of *Innister* decades

14

previously. Ruins remained of *Hammer* (but not *Gorn*), and there also existed knowes (huge earthen mounds) at both places. We often played at these spots in my early childhood.

Other landmarks around the farm did have specific names. *Knock-ha'* was the name given to the hill-slope at the back of *Innister*. Beyond that was *Kevady* (usually pronounced *Kebbidie*), a higher hill-edge, and to the west, the delightfully-termed *Holes o'Nuggle*.

Immediately to the back of the farmhouse was the *bigging*, and behind that the grassy area known simply as *'the green'*. *Innister* never had a flower-garden as such. None of the farms did in those days.

I might be biased, but I've long thought that the view from *Innister* overlooking *Wasbister Loch* and the *Bay o'Saviskaill*, with *Keirfea Hill* rising beyond, and looking right across to the *Head o'Farraclett*, is one of the very finest in the whole of Orkney (and better still from slightly higher up the hill - see cover painting & colour photo section). As bairns, of course, we tended to take the unspoilt scenery for granted. It was all we knew and we failed to appreciate its true beauty. That all changed in later years, when I never failed to visit *Innister* without admiring the striking view.

John Gibson Marwick

The Marwick Name

Marwick is a Norse name, possibly originating from the village and district of Marvik, near Stavanger, in Norway. It has been suggested that Norse settlers first brought the name to the small area of Marwick in Birsay, though Orkney historian, Dr. Hugh Marwick suggests the name might come from a Swedish dialect word of that spelling, meaning *'a shallow bay'* (which aptly describes *Marwick Bay* in Birsay). The extensive family research of my brother, Robert C. Marwick[2] over many years brought him into touch with Marwicks in Canada, USA, Australia, New Zealand and South Africa, as well as many parts of Britain. Nowhere did he find anyone whose ancestry could not be traced back to Orkney. In this country, at least, the name seems most certainly to have originated in Orkney, being well and truly rooted in the island of Rousay.

Knarston

My father, John Gibson Marwick, was born at the farm of *Knarston* in the Sourin district of Rousay in 1885. My grandmother, Betsy Gibson, died of septicaemia shortly after giving birth, aged just twenty-one. My grandfather, George Ritchie Marwick of *Ervadale*, died of tuberculosis just two years later, aged

---

[2] Ever in love with his home island, Robert wrote three books on aspects of Rousay history. His seminal work is the very thoroughly researched, *'Rousay Roots: Family Histories in Rousay, Egilsay, and Wyre'* (1994), a detailed genealogy of most of the families of Rousay, Egilsay & Wyre over several centuries. The book has gone through 3 editions and while now out of print, can be viewed on the website www.rousayroots.com.

Robert's other books are *'From My Rousay Schoolbag'* (1995), a history of schooling on the island from 1725; and the delightful, *'In Dreams We Moor'* (2000), an affectionate 'tour' of the island, weaving in many ageless stories from the near and distant past.

twenty seven. Now an orphan, my father was brought up by his mother's parents.[3]

John Marwick married Anna Craigie in 1910, and they lived at *Knarston* for a few years before purchasing the farm of *Innister*. It was a big day for my dad when he herded his cattle along the road from *Knarston*, up the Sourin hill, and down the *Leean* towards his new home at *Innister*. Here the couple worked hard to make the farm a success, and to provide for their ever-growing family. He was regarded as a first-rate farmer and was well respected in the parish. I was only five when my father passed away, so I have few distinct memories of him. But those I do retain, I remember fondly, and treasure dearly.

Piggy-backing

There was a long table in the kitchen of *Innister*, which took up almost the whole length of one wall. At meal times my father used to sit in the middle of a long bench that stretched along the side of the table. As a toddler, I used to climb up on his back while he was eating dinner.

---

[3] For further, illuminating information on this family situation, see Robert C. Marwick's booklet, '*Our Line: The Marwicks of Innister*', privately published, 2003.

I would sit perched there all the time he ate, and annoying though it must have been for him, especially after a hard morning's work, I never remember him getting annoyed with me or telling me to get down. This, I believe, is the very earliest memory I have of my dad.

One Last Sweetie

Another early memory I retain is of my dad going into Kirkwall on business one morning and coming back later in the day carrying a poke of sweeties for all the bairns. Thankfully there were a lot of sweets in it, as they had to go round a long way. Sweeties were a rare treat for the Marwick bairns, so I was excited at the thought of getting even one. I hastily popped it in my mouth - and boy was it good! Aged ninety, I still remember the flavour – not black cherry, but rather similar – and never since that day have I tasted anything with that distinct taste.

The following day, when I was outside playing at the front of the auld house, I saw the empty poke. For no particular reason I picked it up - and discovered to my enormous delight there was still one lonely sweetie at the bottom of it! This was an extremely rare and precious find. Naturally, I told no-one of my significant discovery, and I enjoyed that last sweet best of all!

Wild Peas

I also preserve precious memories of my father and my brothers being in the harvest field after reaping oats, when they were stooking sheaves. There were some wild peas growing among the oats and as he walked back to the reaper

on one occasion, I asked my dad to pick some peas for me. Busy as he was, he found the time to attend to his wee daughter's earnest pleas, throwing away the shells before handing them to me. Boy, did I enjoy those peas – they tasted delicious! Completely different from frozen peas, garden peas, or anything out of a tin. I ate my fill of wild peas many's the time after that initial taste.

Baby Sister

I distinctly recall, early one morning when I was five, my dad coming upstairs when my sister, Jean and I were still in bed. I mind him standing in the doorway of our bedroom and proudly announcing that his wife had just given birth to another child. Jean and I leapt out of bed in an instant, bounding down the stairs to see our new-born sister, who

19

had been delivered earlier that morning in the ben-room. I had never seen such a cute peedie baby – we were even allowed to cuddle her. She was given the name Nettie, and was the last child to be born to John and Anna Marwick. [4]

Aunt Bella at *Yorville*

I rarely ever saw my mother's only sister, my aunt Isabella, who lived at *Yorville,* near *Hullion,* on the other side of Rousay. But I well recall one particular Sunday when my mother made hasty arrangements to go over to 'visit' her, a five-mile hike one way. I pleaded to be allowed to go with her, but was denied the privilege. I roared and gret. To pacify me, my father took me out for a walk, a rare treat for a child with twelve siblings and such hard-working parents. We walked through the big gate up to the braes of *Knock-ha'* and back. I loved being in my dad's company – the sole recipient of his attention! I only found a great while later that aunt Bella had in fact died that morning, and my mother had gone to *Yorville* to make arrangements for her funeral. Only then did it make sense to me why my mother didn't take me with her.

Illness & Death

My father took ill in November 1932, of pleurisy and pneumonia. I distinctly remember watching from the playground at Wester school as an orangey-brown horse-drawn ambulance, which had crossed over by boat from the

---

[4] *'Peedie'* is perhaps the most common of all Orkney dialect words, and means small. The word is used recurrently throughout this book.

mainland, took my sick father from *Innister*, back up the road and to the pier. That sad sight etched firmly in my little mind, and it remains so to this day. It was the last time I ever saw my dad.

When he was ill in hospital, my mother went to stay for a time with a relative in Kirkwall, so that she could visit him. Their house, *Quandal*, was situated on Thoms Street. It was of course a very worrying time for my mother, as Nettie, who she took with her, was just a baby; I was only five, and Jean was just seven. John Marwick passed away on 1st March the following year, 1933, aged forty-eight, just one day before his wife's fiftieth birthday.

Anna Logie Craigie

Hullion

My mother was Anna Logie Craigie, who came from the Post Office at *Hullion*, in Frotoft. Her father was John Inkster Craigie, Rousay's first sub-postmaster, a role he served for fifty years. Her mother was Mary Sinclair, from *Stennisgorn*, a tiny croft near *Sketquoy*, of which little trace now exists. Born in 1883, my mother lived with her parents and siblings, Isabella (born 1880) and John (born 1884). As a young girl, she got involved in the various duties of the Post Office, which included tapping out Morse code to send telegraph messages to Kirkwall.

Seamstress

My mother also worked from home as a dress-maker (as did her sister, Bella). She worked hard, and used to say that she would get all the housework done as quickly as possible so she could spend the rest of the day sewing clothes. There exists an extant photo of her standing alongside Bella (see photo section) – both women having made the beautiful dresses in that picture. In her younger years my mother was very slim – measuring a mere twenty-two inches round the waist when she married. She sewed a huge amount of clothes in later years, too.

Stray Lambs

As at the Post Office, so too my mother worked extremely hard at *Innister* – especially after my father's death, when she had several young kids to raise and a farm to keep, albeit with the help of several older sons. As well as attending to the housework, for example, she would have to milk the kye and help look after the sheep. I once remember my mother and I trekking all over the stretch of land at the back of *Moan* – a considerable distance across the hill - in search of stray lambs, and bringing them back within the fold. We were out for a long time, and must have walked miles. It got gye dark, and the ground beneath our feet was rough and uneven, but, mission accomplished, we somehow managed to find our weary way home.

The Marwick Family

Phebe

I was born on the 27th March 1927. I was named after a friend of my mother – Phebe Foulis, who lived with her sister, Mary, just off Bridge Street in Kirkwall. Phebe died shortly before my birth, so Mary suggested that my mother might name her daughter after her. I was given her full name - Phebe Marshall Traill Foulis (Marwick) - quite a mouthful! Phebe is a biblical name, often spelt Phoebe, and means *'bright and shining'*, apparently.

Brothers & Sisters

I was born into a big family, being the second-youngest of thirteen children - eight boys & five girls. My siblings were…

John Craigie (known as Johnny or sometimes Jock) - the first-born in the Marwick family, entering the world on the 28th September 1910.[5]

Sydney Sinclair - born a year after Johnny, on 6th November 1911, also at *Knarston,* where my parents were still living at the time.[6]

David Gibson was born two years later, on 28th August 1913.[7]

---

[5] Johnny worked at *Innister* until his marriage to Rita Craigie of *Ivybank* in 1933, whereupon the couple moved to *Brigsend* on Rousay's west side, where Johnny served as foreman on *Westness* farm for many years before settling as tenant farmer at *Mid-Greenigoe*, Orphir in 1945.

[6] After leaving Kirkwall Grammar School, Sydney left Orkney, and was called up to serve in the army during World War 2. In 1942 he married Margaret Sinclair of Wick. The couple settled in the Caithness town & Sydney worked as a teacher of Technical subjects.

[7] David left home after attending KGS, to study Agricultural zoology at Aberdeen University. In 1940 he married Marjorie Merchant from

James Craigie - Jim to all who knew him – was born at the *Hullion* Post Office[8] on 16th May 1915.[9]

Betsy (or Betty) was also born at *Hullion* Post Office, on 31st August 1916.[10]

Roderick's birthday was 25th September 1918 – he was the first child to be born in the 'new' house at *Innister*.[11]

William Lyle (Bill) was born at *Innister* on 12th November 1919.[12]

Anna Logie was born at *Innister* on 26th May 1921.[13]

Fraserburgh. David served in the RAF during the war, and later became headmaster of an agricultural college in Wester Ross.

[8] Although my parents were now settled at *Innister*, my mother returned to her parents at *Hullion* for the birth-giving process.

[9] After leaving Wester school, Jim worked for a while at *Langskaill*, before moving back to farm *Innister* after the death of his father. He married Isabella Lyon of Sourin in December 1947, a month after taking over the stock & implements of *Innister*. He farmed *Innister* till his death in 1972, after which his son, Alistair took over.

[10] Betty attended Wester school, after which she worked at home for several years, later securing domestic jobs at 1 or 2 farmhouses in the district. She also worked for a while at *Swannay* farm in Birsay. But soon her health broke down, and she was diagnosed with Multiple Sclerosis. Betty had a quiet personality and was universally liked.

[11] After leaving school Roderick worked on the farms of *Nearhouse* in Rousay, and *Woodstock* in Holm. He also worked for the firm of *Balfour Beattie* on the construction of the road on the Churchill Barriers. Roderick married Evelyn Clouston of *Tou* in 1945, and the couple later settled in *Cogar*.

[12] Bill worked at home for a considerable time before moving to the Orkney mainland, where he served on a farm near Kirkwall and also at *Swanbister Farm* in Orphir. He later moved to Ayrshire, where he met and married Jean Marshall of Wishaw in 1965.

[13] After leaving Wester school, Anna went to Craibstone College in Aberdeenshire to complete a 1-year course in rural skills. Moving back to Orkney, she worked for a time as a domestic at *Swanbister* farm in Orphir, where she met and later married the farmer's son, Frank Bichan, in 1945. They took over *Crantit Farm* in St Ola shortly after.

Rare photographic sweep of Wasbister, late 1800s (taken by John Logie, butler to General Traill-Burroughs). Foreground, rounding sheep at Langskaill (note the hay-stacks in lower field). The auld house of Innister can be seen in distance (centre), & to front-right of it, Hammer, whose tenants were evicted by Burroughs in the 1880s. (photo courtesy of Tommy Gibson Collection).

My great grandparents, John & Jane Gibson of Knarston, who helped bring up my father after his mother, Betsy, died in childbirth.

My paternal grandfather, George Ritchie Marwick; one of a number of children to be christened after the Rev. George Ritchie, a popular Rousay minister in the 19th century. (photo courtesy of Tommy Gibson Collection).

My grandparents, John and Mary Craigie of Hullion Post Office (seated), along with their offspring, Anna (left, my mother), John & Isabella, c1900.

My mother (left), & her sister, Bella.

My mother as a young woman, working the loom.

Intriguing group photo dated c1916, featuring my great aunt Jessie Gibson (2nd left), David Gibson (5th left), Agnes Corsie, Knarston, who later married my uncle John (6th left), & my father (aged about 31). (photo courtesy of Tommy Gibson Collection).

A very rare photo of a Marwick bairn as an infant. It is in fact me.

One of the few photos of any of the Marwick girls as children; taken outside Swartifield, Back row left to right, Anna, Betty. Front row, Jean, Cora (Gibson), me.

Wester school photo, 1916, showing Sydney, left (aged 5) & Johnny (6). Only 3 school photos were taken over the entire quarter of a century the Marwicks attended school.

Wester school photo 1931, featuring Marwick bairns, Anna, centre; Robert, right; Donald cross-legged on ground (aged 7).

1931 school photo – Bill (top) & Jean (aged 6).

Wester School photo 1939. The 3 pupils in my year were; back row, me, 3rd from right (aged 12), & to my left, Elsie Donaldson & Edwin Moar. My sister, Nettie is front row, 3rd from right (aged 7). The teacher is Miss Sutherland.

11 of the Marwick family, at Nettie's wedding, 1954. Back row - Jim, Johnny, Robert, Bill, Sydney, Donald, Roderick. Front row - Jean, me, Nettie, Anna. Only David & Betty are missing from this family photo.

Above: my brother, David as a young man serving in the Forces.

Below: my dear sister, Betty, who suffered from MS most of her adult life. This photo was taken on our sliver wedding anniversary.

My mother, visiting her daughter, Jean in Fife, summer of '48, just 6 months before her death. Some see a likeness to me in this photo.

Left: For long, the only photo I knew of the fine, handsome man that was my father. My mother proudly hung the framed original in the main room at Innister shortly after his death.

Above & left: Innister farm-house & farm buildings as they looked in my youth.

Left to right, Anna, Jean & me, on my first ever trip to Kirkwall, aged 15.

Later photo of me, in my mid-20s

Robert Craigie was born on 23 December 1922.[14]
Donald Gibson was born on 10th February 1924.[15]
Mary Jane (Jean) was born on the 25th March 1925.[16]
Nettie Orr Gibson was born on 14th November 1932.[17]

[14] After leaving Wester school at age 14, Robert moved to Kirkwall Grammar School, where he gained several Highers. He worked as a counter clerk at the Post Office in Lyness before being drafted into the Army, where he served for four years, 3 of them in India. After being demobbed, Robert gained a degree at Aberdeen University, and trained as a teacher. He moved to Ayrshire, where he met and married Betty Leishman of Stevenson, in 1955.

[15] After leaving school, Donald worked as a farm-hand on farms in South Ronaldsay, Sandwick and St Ola. It was in the 2nd of these parishes that he met local lady, Irene Kirkness, whom he married in 1951. Donald was an avid reader, and also won several prizes in ploughing matches and in sheep-shearing competitions.

[16] Jean attended Wester school, except for her period of stay with her aunt in Sourin, when she attended the school in that parish. She worked at home before getting a job in the Wester school-house, working to Mr & Mrs Miller, with their young family. She also worked for a spell at the Rousay Post Office, to her relatives, the Yorstons. Jean married Leonard Marwick of *Moan* in 1943, and moved to Fife shortly after, where Leonard was called to work as a bricklayer in the mines during the war.

[17] Nettie left Wasbister school to attend KGS, staying with her brother, Johnny and his wife at *Greenigoe* for a time before moving to the Hostel. She attended college at Craibstone, near Aberdeen in 1950-1, studying domestic sciences. Here she was top student for the year. Returning home, she worked for a time as a domestic at *Crantit Farm*, where she met George Laughton of Orphir. The couple married in 1954.

Early Sibling Memories

First Toy Doll

I recall one occasion when I was a child, wanting to go to see my great-aunt Jessie, who lived at *Swartifield* in Sourin, but I wasn't allowed to go. I was very disappointed. My brother Roderick, nine years my senior and known for his aptitude at woodwork, felt sorry for me and went out to the stable, where in no time he carved a small, thin wooden doll (about 4 inches high) out of a piece of wood. I mind it as weel as can be. Roderick handed the doll to me as a consolation-gift. I was over the moon. I had never had a doll before. It was indeed wonderful consolation for not being allowed to go to visit my auntie.

Sweeties fae Sydney

For many years after he left home, my brother, Sydney made sure he came to his native island during the summer holidays to help with the farm work. I remember how hard he worked every time he came home, not least when singling neeps.

Sydney was a smoker in his youth, as were the majority of young men in the days before the lasting health effects of smoking were fully known. One year as a young unmarried man when he came home from Wick, Sydney gave me some money to go down to the shop at *Quoyostray* to buy some cigarettes for him, and a penny to spend on myself. I was delighted, for a penny was a lot of money to a peedie girl in

those days, and I knew that it would buy exactly ten caramels. I walked back to the neep-field where Sydney was working, and handed him his purchases. He turned down the offer of a sweetie.

Then the thought crossed my mind that I should really share my prized booty with my other siblings, most of whom were there in the field, singling neeps. But I realised that, with so many brothers and sisters, if I shared them out, I might have only one, or at most two left for myself. Besides, I had worked for these caramels by trekking down to the shop for my brother; and in any case nobody seemed to be watching, so they perhaps didn't know I had any sweeties. So, shrewdly, I decided to keep my reward a secret, and I happily enjoyed all ten caramels to myself!

Nettie's Lamb

When my sister, Nettie was peedie she owned a wee lamb, of which she was very fond. It followed her everywhere. One day, however, Nettie was ill in bed. Five years older than Nettie, I was out planting some cabbage plants in the garden. I carefully planted them one by one. When at last I was finishing off the last cabbage, I turned round to compliment myself on a job well done. To my horror the only cabbage to be seen was the one I had just finished planting. All the rest had been eaten by Nettie's lamb! Annoyed at my handiwork being so heartlessly destroyed,

I chased after the lamb, which scurried off into the house, taking refuge in the ben room, where Nettie was lying ill. Nettie found the incident highly amusing; I decidedly less so!

Socks for David

My mother continued helping her family in any way she could even long after they had moved away from *Innister*. On one occasion, after knitting a pair of socks for my brother, David, who had moved 'sooth', she parcelled them up and asked me to go and give them to the postman as he passed by the end of *Innister*'s road. I gladly obliged. I waited for postie to arrive at the end of the road on his bike, then dutifully handed him the parcel, remarking as firmly as I knew how, *'Noo, mind on, that's a pair o' socks for David!'*

I felt I needed to provide this information with the expectation that postie would be travelling all the way to Aberdeen to personally deliver the socks to my brother! Aged just six, I wasn't yet fully aware of how Royal Mail operated. Postie laughed out loud, but assured me the parcel would indeed get delivered safely.

Postman Jim

The Wester postie at the time was Jim Craigie, who lived at *Deithe*. He always stopped and spoke with the bairns that

28

came to the end of the road to meet him, also appreciating the fact that he wouldn't have to cycle up the often long farm-roads. (*Innister's* road, for example, was a third of a mile long) He was a fine man, and I liked him. He always left us laughing.

By the time I was in my teens the postmen were using post-vans, which aided them greatly. The Wester postie still had to leave his van at the roadside in certain places where the road going in to houses was just a rough dirt track. This was the case with the long, steep road going up to the houses scattered around *Everybist*. Postie would even have to trek all the way up the hill to *White Meadows* if ever there was a letter for that household – an enormous distance from the main road.

Stranger-Brother

Being one of the eldest in the family, and fourteen years my senior, David was grown up and away from home all the years that I was a child. He left Orkney after leaving school, and didn't come home very often. As a consequence I rarely met my older brother in my youth, and hardly knew

him (a loss I tried to make up for in later years).[18] I do remember him bringing me a wee present on one return visit to *Innister*, when he was accompanied by his fiancée, Marjorie, a native of Fraserburgh. I liked Marjorie a lot (we also shared the same birthday, though she was nine years older). David evidently liked her a lot, too, for he married her soon after.

The Night the House Shook

One night when I was peedie, I was upstairs alone in bed. Jean and Betty, who shared the bedroom with me, were still up and about. It was blowing a howling gale outside - one of the worst I ever remember - and I couldn't get to sleep. Suddenly, there blew such a terrific gust that the house literally shook. I even wondered if it was going to collapse completely! (It didn't; indeed, it's still standing eighty years later!). And although the windows were shut tight, the very bed I was lying in swung several inches to one side. I was petrified – too afraid even to get up and run downstairs to my mum and sisters. I've had a right fear of strong winds ever since.

---

[18] This was cut short in 1973 when my brother was killed in a tragic car accident, while travelling as HM Inspectorate of Schools in Moray.

Auld Pat

When Nettie was peedie, she had some nicknames for those siblings whose names she found impossible to pronounce. The letter 'J' she found especially problematic (as, it has been observed, do many adult Orcadians!). Thus, Jim she called '*Pim*', Johnny was '*Sonnie*' and Jean was '*Teen*'! But the rest of us didn't escape her misnomers either. Roderick, for example she called '*Ackie*', and Donald was – '*Yap-yap*'! I'm not going to tell what name she had for me!

On one of those rare occasions when my mother fell ill, the G.P. was called. The doctor in Rousay at the time was the long-serving Dr Paterson, or '*Auld Pat*' as he was colloquially (and not very flatteringly) known. When he came into the kitchen to see my mother, Nettie ran through to the bedroom, shouting, '*Mum, Auld Pat's here*', in full ear-

shot of the doctor! Mother was sore embarrassed, and Dr Paterson probably was, too, though he never said a word.

Dr Paterson was the only doctor on the island, being assisted by a resident nurse, Nurse Park. I also recall Dr Bannerman, the Medical Officer of Health, who was based in Kirkwall, but who came out to Rousay once a year to do medical checks on all the bairns at school. Though the occasion was hardly one of great merriment, it did provide a welcome diversion from classwork!

'Peedie Hooses' at the Quarry

Jean, Donald and I – all fairly close to each other in age – would often go and play '*Peedie Hooses*' at the quarry by the dam, to the west-side of *Innister*. Our '*hooses*' were wee sheltered coves that were cut into the rock-surface. With natural stone ledges ideal for kitchen shelves, these were perfect for playing in. What fun we had up there!

My mother used to buy her tea-sets from a mail-order firm in Bristol. Once she got sent home a set of six small coffee cups. Being so tiny as to be of no practical use, we were overjoyed when she 'donated' them to our '*hooses*'. On an earlier occasion, I broke a handle off a cup at *Innister*. Realising it was no longer any use in the house, mum told me I could have it for our '*peedie hooses*', but as a form of punishment, sent me up to the quarry with it right away. Reluctantly, I went out the door with the cup, but in next to no time returned, empty handed. '*Where have you been?*' my mother asked. '*To the quarry*', I replied, innocently. '*What a lie!*' my mother retorted, knowing full well I hadn't been out of the house long enough to get even half-way to the quarry and back. Sure enough, I had gone out and simply thrown the broken cup at the back of the house. I got a good smack for telling a downright lie (the only time, incidentally, that I ever remember getting a skelping at home).

Mischief on Berriebrae

There was a hillside up at the back of *Innister* known as *Berriebrae*, and it was covered with blackberry bushes. The Marwick bairns used to love trooping up to this secluded spot at various times every summer, usually on a Sunday morning. Each with our own jar, we would collect berries to take back to our mother, who would wash them and sprinkle them on top of her creamy rice pudding, which she made for desert most Sundays. Everyone found this totally delicious, especially we bairns, who had helped provide the topping.

On one occasion, I was unable to go along with my brothers and sisters, so Donald lovingly informed me he would take my jar and fill it up with berries for me. Off they set, and after a couple of hours returned home, delighted with their 'catch'. All the jars were filled with berries. Donald handed me mine, and I immediately picked a berry and stuck it in my mouth.

But something was wrong. It didn't remotely taste like the juicy blackberries I had savoured so often before. As I quickly realised, it wasn't a berry at all! My brother Donald, aged just seven or eight himself, had played a devious trick on his peedie sister. Just for fun (fun?), he had filled my jar with sheep droppings instead of berries. I was too young and naïve to recognise the difference. On realising what I had just put in my mouth, my face screwed up in contortions and I instantly spat out the feigned 'berry'. *'Did-dad, seep sit'*, I uttered, disgustedly (*'Gid-gad, sheep s**t'* – *'gid-gad'* being an Orcadian expression of disgust). Perhaps not surprisingly, virtually all my siblings found the incident highly amusing. Perhaps equally unsurprisingly, I most certainly didn't!

Lost Half-Crown

One day Roderick gave me half-a-crown to go down to the van and buy a pack of cigarettes. I sauntered down *Innister's* road, observing that the van was still standing at the end of the road of the neighbouring farm, *Furse*. I got about two thirds down the farm road when I noticed the van leaving *Furse*. For some reason I took fright, thinking I would miss it. Instead of moving faster towards the end of the road, I threw away the half-crown in a panic, turned round and ran all the way back to *Innister*!

Naturally Roderick was somewhat surprised at my early arrival back at the house – not least to find that I was carrying neither his much longed-for fags nor the hard-earned cash he gave me to pay for them! However, despite having lost a whole half-crown (a considerable sum to a hard-working young man), Roderick seemed to understand that I had acted in genuine fright, and remarkably, didn't lose his temper with me for my moment of utter madness (although it was some time before he trusted me with his cash again!)

'Batchie', 'Grab' & 'Please & Thank You'!

The Marwick bairns enjoyed simple forms of entertainment. Many of us received the gift of a Jews Harp (or trump as it was known), and we enjoyed strumming away on that. Another favourite recreation was cards. Everyone at *Innister* played cards; as bairns we played cards many's an evening – three or four of us together. There wasn't much else to do at nights after all the long day's work was done (although I also knitted a lot). Favourite games were *'Batchie'* (an old Scottish card-game), *'Grab'* (more commonly known as *'Snap'*), and *'Please & Thank you'*.

I mind that Donald was rather competitive when it came to card-playing. He always liked to win, and would go to almost any length to ensure such outcome! As we played *'Please & Thank you'* - my favourite card game of all - we had to request cards from each other according to the rules of the game. We had to rely a lot on memory, seeking to remember what cards other folk had. This was simply impossible to do in regard to Donald, for night after night, as we were about to play, my brother would grab an old orange-box that we had at *Innister*, and set it on the table. He would then insist on keeping his cards hidden behind the orange-box as the game proceeded, so we couldn't even see how many cards he had, let alone guess what they might consist of! No exhortation on our part would induce him to remove his hand from behind that darn box. No wonder he won so often! But it was all in fun – even if my brother took it rather seriously – and we all thoroughly enjoyed the games we played together, orange-box or not!

To a lesser extent we also played chequers, but not tiddleywinks or other 'fancy' games, which few families owned in those days.

I wasn't much of a reader – books weren't so readily available in my childhood, and reading wasn't so positively encouraged in the way it is nowadays. But I do remember proudly owning a copy of *'Alice in Wonderland'* and *'Alice Through the Looking-Glass'*, both of which I won as school prize-books.

My family owned a radio, which stood on a chiffonier just inside the ben door, but it was mainly used to listen to the news. However, I do recall that when one of my brothers came in for dinner each lunchtime, he would switch on the radio. All the while he ate his dinner, he would listen to *'Housewives Choice'*, which played the most popular music of the day.

Wasbister School

Hot chocolate

I got two teachers at different times during my years at Wester school – Miss Matheson and Miss Sutherland – as well as a third, who taught us when one of the main teachers was off.

Pupils would walk to school from their various Wester homes in all weathers. During the winter months we would relish the privilege of warming ourselves by the old black stove before lessons began. During these months also, most bairns brought tubs of cocoa to school, along with a supply of sugar and milk. At lunchtime, the teacher would boil the kettle on the stove, then fill our mugs with hot water to make a delicious mug of cocoa. Boy did I enjoy that hot drink, especially on cold wintry days!

School Lunch

Come the summertime, my friends and I would sit outside at lunchtime, under the school dyke, eating our 'pieces', which often included a pancake and butter, or bread and jam. Everything tasted good when you were young and hungry! The food would be washed down with milk from a small bottle, also taken from home each day. Bairns who lived near the school usually went home for lunch. Along with one or two others, I often accompanied Renie to her home at nearby *Maybank* during lunch-hour. Renie's parents, Eleen and Mackie, would be sitting eating dinner at the table by the open fire. I could never understand how they put up with a band of chattering, giggling girls storming into their home each lunchtime, but they did!

Pin-Prick

During winter-time, my class used to sit in a semi-circle round the big school stove for lessons. One day at dinner-time, when the teacher was through in the adjoining school-house, we bairns sat sipping our cocoa and eating our 'pieces' around the fire. All at once, and for no particular reason, I jumped from my seat and went over to Elsbeth, several years older than myself, and stuck a pin into her

backside. Before I had a chance to pull it out again, Elsbeth jumped up in pain and darted off across the room, the pin still securely attached to her derriere! I can't recall if I ever apologised for my unwitting action (I think not!), but thankfully it proved to have no long-term adverse effect on my friendship with Elsbeth.

Clean Slate

Wester bairns didn't have jotters in those days, though we did use paper copy-books to learn to write. For everything else we used slate-pencils and slate-boards set in a wooden frame (only the teacher used chalk for her blackboard). The slate-stick screeched horribly every time you wrote with it.

Arithmetic, or sums as it was then called, I sometimes found particularly difficult. One day when engaged in this exercise, I turned round in my seat and noticed that the boy sitting behind me, George o'*Sketquoy*, a couple of years younger than myself, had completed all the sums the class was given to do. His slate was full, while mine was bare – I simply didn't know the answers. In a fit of spontaneous jealousy, I grabbed the bottle of water on George's desk –

provided for each pupil along with a cloth so they could wipe their slate clean after each use - and poured it over George's slate, instantly wiping the answers off his board.

George was horrified, as was the teacher, who I always felt didn't really like me anyway (she had her favourites). By way of punishment, she gave me nine pages of geography from the school-book to learn before the following morning. This was an awful lot for a young girl to memorise, and I knew I wouldn't be able to. Sure enough, next morning I was unable to answer the teacher's questions. For this failure, I was given the belt, the only time I was ever meted this form of punishment during all my years at school.

I ever after felt that the teacher got it wrong. Yes, I deserved the belt, but not for being unable to memorise nine pages of geography, which was a bit much for any seven-year-old. What I should have been punished for, I felt, was my initial crime – pouring water over smart-alec George's slate. In truth I liked George, and we never fell out over the incident.

Memorising the Bible

Even as a young boy, my brother, Donald, worked hard at *Innister* – for example he regularly fed the kye before setting off for school each morning. He was regarded as a bright pupil – in particular he had a great memory. The bairns got a Bible story at school every day. As Jean, Donald and I walked to school each morning (in the summer months Donald walked barefoot), my brother

would remind me of the previous day's Bible story, in case I got asked a question on it. Donald was so good to me, and I was so thankful for my brother's retentive memory! I rarely remembered the Bible story – but then I was younger than Donald. I always felt I had a memory like a sieve – both as a youngster and in later life (even though I can mind childhood stories like these as weel as can be).

Sunday School

There was no church in Wester at the time, but a Sunday School was held every Sabbath in the school. My mother encouraged as many of her offspring to attend as possible. I was one who went. The service was taken by Jeemy Low, a really fine, pious man, well-advanced in years, and bent forward with a bad back, the effects of rheumatism after years of hard toiling in the massive garden at *Westness House* on the island's Westside, where he served as gardener. But he was nevertheless so committed to teaching Bible truths that he walked all the way from his *Westness* home to lead the meetings in Wester every Sunday. Afterwards, of course, he would have to trek all the way home, often in the dark.

Jeemy used to organise a Sunday School picnic at *Westness House,* Wester pupils being transported there on the back of a horse and cart – a great novelty in itself. The picnics were well-attended, not least because monetary prizes awarded for the races were greater than the prizes given for the local school picnic! Following the races and games, tea and goodies were served. After this, Jeemy would give his pupils a tour of *Westness House* gardens. This was sheer delight to all the bairns, for the gardens were enormous and beautifully maintained. The main attraction, however, was the innumerable trees that towered above pupils on every side. Rousay, like much of Orkney, was largely treeless, and so most bairns had never seen a real tree before, let alone what seemed like a near-forest! To top it all, this dream garden was even home to a large peacock, which proudly spread its multi-coloured wings for all the ecstatic bairns to gaze at in wonder.

Four Dolls

One of my school teachers had younger twin sisters. These siblings owned lots of celluloid dolls – an early form of plastic. I remember her bringing four dolls to school for the bairns to play with (the twins were grown up by this time), along with whole boxes of dolls' clothes. How my friends and I enjoyed dressing these dolls – all the more so because we didn't have anything of the kind at home. I always thought it was so good of the teacher to donate them to the school for our pleasure.

'S't'chr'!

One of my teachers had a habit of nipping in to the school-house, where she lived, during class-time. Naturally, we bairns would get up to all sorts of mischief while she was away. Invariably, someone would cry out, *'Here's teacher!'* - usually in shortened form, *'S't'chr!'* – even when, half the time, this wasn't the case. It wasn't in fact difficult to know when the teacher really was on her way back to the classroom – for she had to pass several windows in order to do so. Everyone saw her coming, and we made sure we were seated nicely at our desks with our heads down when she came in.

Knitting

I did knitting at school and excelled at this activity. Once, when my regular knitting was finished (I was always the first to do so), the teacher asked me to knit a pair of booties for her recently-born nephew, Edgar. I was only five or six years old at the time, but I agreed to knit the booties (I had little choice!). I was given the wool at school on the Friday and began knitting them that same evening. My mother helped with knitting the heels. I beavered away, and remarkably, had the socks finished by Monday morning. I remember the teacher looking the socks over and complimenting me on my achievement, saying 'Isn't she just fifty' (meaning, isn't she really clever – a phrase I never heard again in my life). The socks were duly forwarded to Edgar's parents, who particularly appreciated the surprise gift from a schoolgirl so tender in years.

Pass the Baby!

Edgar's parents in fact received the booties that same Monday, as they happened to be staying on holiday with the teacher in the school-house. It was decided to give the kids a treat by allowing us to see the wee baby. So his mother passed him in to the teacher through the class-room window, to save her from walking right round the school building to the main entrance. The window was held open by a large chalk-board duster, acting as a makeshift window-jam. I couldn't help thinking what a disaster it might be if the duster got knocked out of place while the baby was being passed in or out of the room! Thankfully, that outcome never occurred, and we were charmed by the cuteness of baby Edgar as he sat proudly on teacher's knee for adoring pupils to view.[19]

School Walks

I recall at least twice going on a school walk from Wester school. We didn't go too far – just down to *Saviskaill* beach. Here we would have a picnic – paid for, most generously, out of the teacher's own pocket, for there were no school funds to provide for such activities. A woman who lived in the vicinity used to meet the school party at the shore, and spend time with them, mainly for the purpose of having a good blether with the teacher. She would sit down on a rock by the shore as she chatted, and I mind some of the boys having a good giggle on discovering that, with her legs spread apart, they could easily see her pink bloomers!

---

[19] Edgar (Gary) Gibson went on to be Head teacher of Art at Kirkwall Grammar School, also becoming well-known as a prominent local artist.

My brother, Robert recalled one school walk to the beach, where the teacher used to select large round stones and make the pupils carry one each all the way back to the school-house. This was to decorate the teacher's garden! I never had to do this, but clearly remember my class having to weed the teacher's garden during school hours on a Friday afternoon. For this service, however, we were awarded a square of chocolate and a ha'penny each, a most generous payment - if only we owned just one other ha'penny to rub against it!

Our teacher was good to us in other ways too. Still a single woman, she sometimes held social gatherings in the school-house on a Saturday night. Once there was some trifle left over, so she gave each of us some on a saucer on the Monday. Any distraction from lessons was welcome, but getting trifle at school we likened to manna from heaven!

Tasty Snack

As we wended our way home from school, my friend Evelyn (later my sister-in-law, for she married my brother, Roderick) and myself often used to pinch a neep from

Innister's field. We hadn't eaten since lunchtime, so would now be quite peckish. We weren't stupid, and chose a spot near the bottom of *Innister's* road, just where there's a dip in the field. In this way we knew that *Innister's* folk couldn't see us. We would pull the neep from the ground, then break off the root using a sharp stone on the dyke by the roadside. Then we would sit under the dyke and peel the swede with our teeth and eat the flesh inside, scraping it out. We would choose a small

neep, so that we could eat it all, and so not waste it. It was surprisingly juicy and tasty, and we found it an irresistible treat - a snack we could eat between meals without ruining our appetite!

I even remember the course of conversation between Evelyn and I on one such occasion while snacking in the neep-field. Trying to act grown-up, one of us would say, '*Damn it, I don't swear!*' The other would reply likewise, '*Damn it, I don't swear 'ither!*' What fun we enjoyed together – little kids, acting big.

Prize Giving

I was only very rarely absent from school during my childhood, so when the minister came to award prizes on Prize Giving Day each November, I was one of those commended for good attendance. The Rev. Davidson would give a presentation first – one year he brought along a collection of exotic items from Africa's Gold Coast - photographs, native hand-carved wooden stools & combs, woven blankets or cloaks and a huge snakeskin. How he got hold of them all I have no idea, but we were fascinated by these rare exhibits from half a world away. The minister told us of the vegetation, and the insect and animal life in that distant land. He spoke of the work done by the missionaries, both educational and religious, and pointed out the advantages that we children in Rousay possessed compared with those in more primitive nations.

It was also during the winter of each year that the minister made a point of visiting all the homes in Wester – dropping in for an evening to each home. Families were given advance notice - for this was one of the most significant visits of the year, and everyone wanted to ensure their house was well cleaned and dusted before the minister's arrival. At *Innister*, the Reverend was ushered into the sitting room at the ben-end and offered freshly brewed tea poured into my mother's finest china tea-set. The Marwicks all liked the man, and didn't at all mind sitting round the peat-fire yarning away with him in polite conversation.

Further Education

Towards the close of their various times at Wester school, the teacher encouraged my mother to send one or two of her more studious children for several years' further study at Kirkwall Grammar School. This was a major decision for my mother to make because the commitment in each case would be for three or four years' duration, the tuition fees were high and she could ill afford it. It was said that at the very most only every second or third child could go, for the other siblings had to stay home and work to pay for him or her to be there. Indeed, only a very small percentage of children from the isles went to Kirkwall Grammar School in those days. But my mother wanted the very best for her bairns, and if they were capable of furthering their education with the view to obtaining better careers, then she intended to do everything in her power to make it happen.

So over the course of many years, my three brothers, Sydney, David and Robert (and much later, my sister, Nettie) were each sent to study in Kirkwall.[20] There was no school hostel in Kirkwall in those early years, so my mother found private accommodation for her boys with a Mainland family in Victoria Street. Sydney and David's secondary schooling overlapped to a degree, so they stayed together in the same digs for a year or two.

I mind my mother having to rise as early as 3 o'clock every Monday morning, and doing a huge baking – enough to last whatever son was in Kirkwall at that time for the entire week. For she knew her sons had big appetites! The food would be packed neatly into boxes, which one of my other brothers would take by horse-and-cart to the Rousay pier, in time for the six o'clock sailing. Arriving on the mainland, the food-boxes would then get transported to Kirkwall, where the recipient Marwick scholar would gratefully collect them and take them back to his digs.

Soon after Nettie moved to the Grammar school at the age of fourteen, she was one of thirty-six girls granted the privilege of staying in the newly-opened schoolgirls' hostel on Old Scapa Road. For some time, facilities were very basic, with meals being meagre in quantity and often

---

[20] It was intended that Anna go on to the Grammar School too, but my mother took ill with heart problems while Anna was staying at *Swartifield*, and she was called back to help at home.

unappetizing. Matters weren't helped by the austere regulations under which the hostel was managed. There were rules for everything, and they were strictly enforced. Each pupil was also given a long list of clothes and other items they were required to obtain before moving to the hostel. In all, my mother spent an additional £15 on clothes for her daughter (extra to all she had already provided for her, and which she had considered more than adequate).[21]

Christmas Concert

In-and-oot the Window

Christmas was a magical time of year for the kids at Wester school, and preparations were begun early in December to rehearse for the Christmas concert, a show put on for Wester folk every year. Decorations and balloons lined the school walls. A platform surrounded by curtains was set up at one end of the room, leaving a very small assembly area for the

children. When the bairns needed to dress-up in special costumes, we had to do this in the school-house, located next door. Access to the school-house was slightly problematic, however, without going out the main door, which would involve being seen by the audience.

---

[21] See also *'Regulations Must be Observed!: Life in a 1950s School Hostel'*, by Berth M. Fiddler, Kirkwall 2013.

So pupils had to clamber through a small window at the side of the stage, and then proceed to the school-house. Such operation had to be carried out as quietly as possible – so as not to disturb the adult audience in the hall. This, of course wasn't always achieved, for we bairns found the peculiar operation a hilarious adventure!

The Demise of *Gloria*

One year, as Christmas approached, I needed a doll for a play that my class was doing at the concert. At the time I didn't own a doll, but my sister, Nettie, had recently been given one as a present – named *Gloria* - and she allowed me to use it for the sketch. The concert went well and afterwards came the dance. I remember walking home late from the Wester school around two in the morning along with my mother and other family members. When we got home, I laid the doll on the couch and went to bed, utterly exhausted.

When I got up the following morning, *Gloria* was no longer on the sofa. One of the farm dogs had chewed the doll (through not my favourite canine, *Peter*, who I knew would never have done such a thing). *Gloria* lay in a mess on the floor. I was distraught that the doll my sister had so kindly loaned me was now torn to shreds and completely unusable. Clearly I had a bit of explaining to do to Nettie when she surfaced that morning!

Nettie's Solo Act

Each Christmas, for the school concert, the teacher tried to ensure that every pupil played a part. One year, a role had been given to everyone – except, that is, for wee Nettie, who in any case was very young, only having recently started school. So that she wouldn't feel left out, the teacher accorded her a small solo act. After several other sketches had been enacted, Netty walked gingerly onto the stage, and pointing to one side of the hall, declared, *'Behold, a spider on the wall – Ladies and gentlemen, that is all!'* Her act over, young Nettie proudly walked off stage. Thoroughly amused at her capable, albeit extremely short-lived theatrical performance, everyone applauded, and Nettie was well chuffed with her achievement.

Santa's in Wester!

When the concert was over the children would wait in great anticipation for the arrival of Santa, who so arranged his hectic world-wide schedule to arrive at Wester school just at the close of the concert! Soon there would be a knock at the door and Santa would appear, to the enormous excitement of every child present.

I recall one such occasion when I was very peedie. I think I may not even have been school age at all, for all the bairns in the Wester district were invited, including pre-schoolers, and a great many came. I was probably four or five. Everyone was up to high-doh waiting for Santa to appear. Finally one of the grown-ups came in and announced that Santa would soon be making an appearance, for he had seen his sledge coming down the brae over *Innister*. *'Innister'*! I thought. *'My own home'!* To think that Santa and his reindeer were passing by *Innister*! What an exciting image! There was a commotion in the lobby – Santa had arrived. There he was – standing in the doorway – an old man in a bright red coat, with white whiskers and a great bulging pack on his back, full of presents. The real Santa! I can recall to this very day how utterly thrilled I was by it all.

The Wasbister District

Nearby Dwellings

The nearest houses and farms to *Innister* were *Tou*, and just beyond it, *Hammerfield*. In *Tou* lived two generations of couples with the same name - auld Annabella and Jeemo, along with young Annabella and Jeemo, and also Evelyn and Edna. Young Jeemo was always referred to as Peemo. Between *Innister* and *Tou* lay the uninhabited croft of *Breckan*, which was used as a stable and byre when I was young.

To the other side of *Innister* was *Furse.* Here lived John Craigie (or Jock o'*Furse* as he was known) and his wife Annie, along with family – really fine neighbours. I mind visiting them one day, and, to my surprise and delight, being offered a plate of strawberries from their garden. We didn't grow strawberries at *Innister*, and I hadn't tasted them before. But they looked delicious, and I couldn't wait to savour. If this wasn't treat enough, Annie came with a great jug of cream, which she lavishly poured onto the scrumptious berries. I heartily stuck into them with the spoon provided – but was instantly repulsed. The cream was sour! Not just slightly off (in those pre-refrigerator days we were used to milk and cream that was a bit off). No, this cream was seriously sour, to the extent that I simply couldn't eat it. Dear Annie wasn't aware or she would never have served it. I set the plate aside saying I wasn't hungry – all the while savouring those beautiful strawbs! I had to wait quite some time before getting the chance to sample this delicacy again.

Beyond *Furse* was the farm of *Sketquoy* (pronounced *Sket-wi*) - the most northerly farm in Rousay. Here lived the Sinclair family. I remember being at *Sketquoy* only once, and that was to a wedding in their barn when I was fourteen.

Along the road, in *Cogar* lived brother and sister, Bobby & Mary-Anne, and next to that, *Ivybank*, home to the Craigie family. Way up the hillside along a track between these two houses were a whole cluster of old cottages, including *Ploverha, Shalter, The Garret, Lingro* and *Giddystall* (each with a delightful Norse name).[22] Some of these places were still inhabited in my

---

[22] Or how about other wonderful Rousay place-names, like *Pow, Cubbidy, Digro, Cruar, Gripps, Clumpy, Rinyo, Gruithen, Whome, Gurnadee*, etc. For the original meaning of these and scores of other Rousay place-names, see the well-researched, *'Place Names Of*

youth, but other than *Everybist*, they are now all completely deserted.

White Meadows

Higher up on the hillside still, on the western slopes of *Keirfea Hill*, and approaching the wonderfully-named *Loch o'Wheethamo*, was the house known as *White Meadows*, so named, apparently, because of the mass of white cotton that used to flourish there. Two elderly brothers and a sister lived there (Jeemo, Fredo and Lizzie Leslie). Fredo was partially blind, and had been all his life. Located high up on the hill, but with a striking view, their house was a long distance from any other dwelling in Wester, and they rarely saw anyone except during the peat-cutting season, when many locals passed-by on their way to the peat-banks.

Every other day Fredo would wend his way down the track to the main road near *Langskaill,* turn left and walk along the road, and up to *Hammerfield*, where relatives of his lived, and where he got a bottle of milk to keep his household going for a day or two. He would walk back home in the late afternoon. It was indeed a very long walk - we often used to meet him on his homeward trek on our way home from school.[23]

Rousay' (1947) by Rousay-born scholar, Hugh Marwick (later OBE). A former headmaster of Kirkwall Grammar School and Director of the Orkney Education Committee, Marwick's other books include 'The Orkney Norn' (1929) and 'Orkney Farm-Names' (1952).

[23] I mind once when Evelyn & I were joking with John o'*Feolquoy*, a few years younger than us. Approaching us on the road, Fredo thought we were harassing the lad, and he came at us, waving his stick in the air. 'Let da peedie boy be!' he shouted. 'Let da peedie boy be!'

Early one morning my brother, Jim, came across an old man standing helplessly at the back of the dam to the west of *Innister*. It was Fredo. It seems he had lost his way en route to *Hammerfield* the previous day, and had spent many hours wandering about – having no idea where he was. Jim kindly helped him on his way back home. This was my first experience of seeing a man *'dotting'* (showing signs of dementia), and remarkably, my only experience during all my twenty years on Rousay. For, compared to today, and for whatever reason, dementia was a very rare illness on the island in those days.

Quoyostray

Just across from *Tou*, there was a small shop at the farm of *Quoyostray* – just a hut joined on to the end of the house. I walked there around ten one morning to buy some food item. I would have been about fourteen or so. I was just about to knock on the house door, when all of a sudden it flew open. Mattie, the shopkeeper was stood there with the large family tea-pot in hand. Not realising that I was standing at the bottom of the steps outside,

she hurled out the contents of the pot – half a pot of hot brewed tea came flying straight into my face before I had the slightest chance of ducking out of the way. The hot tea, of course, stung my face, and soaked my clothes. As soon as she realised what she had done, Mattie was horrified, and quickly ran for a towel to help clean my face and clothes. I walked back to *Innister* trying to assess the odds against such an occurrence, and hoping nobody at home was going to ask if I was offered a cup of tea at *Quoyostray*!

Moan

Way up across the hill to the west of *Innister* was *Moan*, where another family of Marwicks lived (far-out relatives). Hugh o'*Moan* was a cobbler, and many's the time I used to walk up across the hillside to *Moan* to get family shoes mended. (My father was a skilled cobbler too, and formerly always repaired the family's footwear).

I always thought Hugh was a fine old man. His wife, Mary, died years before him (I vaguely remember her – slender and dressed in black). Hugh's house being situated high up on the hillside and far away from other dwellings, it was a lonely place for him to live and work. (His two sons, Tommy and Leonard[24], worked in

---

[24] Leonard later married my sister, Jean, and continued his father's trade as a cobbler for many a year after he left Orkney.

Kirkwall, but often came back home at weekends). Greatly appreciating company, Hugh used to insist that I sit down and yarn with him while he sat repairing shoes. I always obliged. People came to him from miles around to mend their footwear – he was known to be very good at his trade.

Collecting for Charity

Occasionally school pupils were sent out to go house-to-house collecting for a popular charity. Usually this task was appointed to my friends, Evelyn and Renie, whom I knew to be the teacher's favourites. But on one rare occasion, I was picked to be Evelyn's partner. We walked to all the houses in the Wester district – a very time-consuming process as there were long track-roads going in to some of the houses and farms. Such was definitely the case with *Moan*, located high up on the hill, to which a long dirt road, not very well kept, wound its way from near *Grain* on the main road. It was the only time I ever recall being on that road, as I usually walked to *Moan* directly over the hill from *Innister*. It was a long walk just to collect a few pennies – and it was never guaranteed that the folk would be home, or that they'd offer to give anything.

Thankfully Hugh o'*Moan* was home, and he happily put a penny or two in the can. Half-way back down the track road, Evelyn and I stopped to count our offerings. It added up to a certain round amount, with a penny or ha'penny above. Deciding it was better to have a round sum, we threw away the extra coin (rather, even, than keep it to ourselves!), before taking our

charity tin back to the teacher at school. I later laughed at our decision to throw money away. It was something I never ever did again in my life!

Quandal & The Lobust

The Geos

The vast gently-sloping moorlands separating *Innister* from the northern shores of Rousay are known as the *Brings*, and they essentially formed *Innister*'s 'back garden' - a vast playground for the Marwick youngsters. Features of this almost totally unspoilt area were especially familiar to me in my childhood, including the *Lobust*, an impressive vertical rock-stack similar to *Yesnaby* castle and the *Old Man of Hoy*, located elsewhere in Orkney. The *Lobust*, being perhaps even less accessible than these others, is far-less known and much-less visited. Further to the west is *Hellia Spur*, Rousay's highest cliff.

There are also a surprising number of *geos* (long, narrow, steep-sided clefts in the cliffs) around the shores of the *Brings*. These include *Icygeo, Quoygeo* and *Mesmesgeo*. There's also a geo at the back of *Sketquoy*, known as '*Stinkaniegeo*' – presumably because of the smell that rises up from the mass of seaweed that collects at the bottom of the cliffs there. (See colour photo section for photos of the Brings, the Lobust and a nearby geo).

Birds' Eggs

Like most teenagers, my brothers enjoyed a bit of a dare, and one means they discovered was to go searching for birds eggs at the cliffs near the *Lobust*. These cliffs have long been a haven for many types of bird, including herring gulls, cormorants, arctic skuas, oystercatchers and puffins. This activity the boys engaged in mainly for a bit of sport, for hens' eggs were aplenty at *Innister*. Nevertheless, they often brought the eggs home, to boil them and enjoy a well-earned treat.

Hanging by a Thread

On one occasion a ship went adrift in bad weather off the north coast of Rousay, releasing a cargo of wooden battens, which came ashore by the *Lobust*. The boys from *Innister* were quick on the scene. Sydney and Jim lowered a daring Roderick over the sheer cliff edge by rope. Being out of their sight, they had no idea their brother was in fact spinning round and round at the end of the rope as he was being lowered. Once on the rocks, the battens had to be raised a few at a time. It wasn't long before Roderick noticed that the rope was starting to give way. By the time it came to raising himself, it was so frayed there was only one strand remaining. He was hauled over the edge just in time - a lucky escape for the lad, who might otherwise have fallen to his death. In actual fact, Roderick's balance was so impaired by the whole experience that he was unable to ride his bike for several weeks afterwards.

Sunday Stroll

Work-wise the Sabbath was observed by everyone on Rousay. Nothing but essential duties, such as feeding the kye and mucking the byre, were performed on this day. Sometimes on a fine Sunday, just to pass the time, I would go for a walk up to the *Lobust* - a fair trek in itself. From there

I would walk along the edge of the cliffs – being careful not to go to close - past *Hellia Spur*, as far west as Quandal, and then directly across the moors and hill home to *Innister* again (thus forming a triangular route). It was a lonely walk, but I enjoyed the peace and quiet. There still lay many ruins of old habitations that ran down through the Quandal district, the remains of a sizeable community that had been wiped out following the notorious Rousay clearances of the mid-1800s.[25] I mind the old Quandal school, too, whose ruins lay by the side of the main road. You can still see them to this day.

Candle-Wax Galore

One January morning in 1937, when I was nine, huge barrels of wax were found washed up on Quandal shore,

---

[25] For more on these sad and disturbing events, see W. P. L. Thomson's gripping, pioneering study, *'The Little General and the Rousay Crofters'*, Edinburgh 1981.

having come from a boat that had run aground.[26] This was the *Johanna Thorden*, a 5,500 ton vessel laden with general cargo worth £2 million pounds, en route from America to Sweden, although the Marwicks knew nothing of these details at the time.[27] Word soon spread about the barrels, and folk flocked to the shore to claim their share of the booty. Being one of the closest dwellings to Quandal, *Innister's* men were among the first to arrive on the scene and claim their portion of the wax.

They rolled the barrels up onto the shore, then loaded as many crates as possible onto a cart. This was pulled by horse over the hill to *Innister*. The wax was stored in a porch at the

---

[26] Occasionally, too, during my stay at *Swartifield*, I used to see great planks of wood washed up in the bay beneath the *Leean* as I walked to and from school.

[27] Nor did they know that all but 5 of the near 40 crew and passengers on board lost their lives as a result of the tragic accident (Indeed, I heard these details for the first time many decades later). The ship ran aground off Swona, south of Orkney's mainland, but cargo and other debris was found on beaches in various parts of Orkney in subsequent days, including South Rondaldsay, Orphir, Stronsay and Westray (See also, Keith Allardyce, '*Found: Beachcombing in Orkney*', Kirkwall 2012).

back of the auld farm-house, and served various purposes on the farm, lasting a long time. Some of my brothers fashioned long wooden candle-stick holders by hand, and they poured molten wax into these frames, adding a piece of string to form a wick. They would make around a dozen candles at a time, all for use at home.

The wax was also used to light *Innister*'s fire each day – it was really good for this purpose and you needed so little of it.[28]

Special Occasions

Wasbister Picnic

Picnics were regularly held in Wester each summer, always at the end of June, on the Friday before the school closed. Children would run races, play games, etc. It was a fun day out for all the family - there being races for the adults too.

During my childhood, the three school picnics on the island – Wasbister, Frotoft and Sourin, were always held at the respective schools, even though the constrictions of the Wester school playground made running races a bit awkward. Formerly, indeed just a few years before I started school, the Wester picnics were always held in a field; eg, at *Knock-ha'* above *Innister*, at *Lee* above *Langskaill* or on the braes above *Cogar*.

---

[28] Paraffin-burning Tilley lamps were generally used for lighting in the house. They were attached to the ceiling and lowered by pulley-rope. I used to love sitting in the grimleens until necessity drove us to light the Tilley. This took some time, for they first had to be re-filled with paraffin. A storm lantern was used to go out to the byres at night, and on other special occasions.

The picnic was a big event, and my mother used to go to great lengths to make sure all her children had decent clothes to wear, in particular plimsoles for the bairns to run the races in. One year she faithfully dressed all the young ones to be ready for the event. There were a lot of us to see to, and she also had all the other work of the farm to attend to. After seeing to everyone, which seemed to take forever, my mother was simply too exhausted to go to the picnic herself, even though it was one of the biggest events in the Wester calendar and she had been really looking forward to it. All the rest of us went – but she felt no option but to stay home and rest.

At the start of the races, all the bairns were given what seemed like an enormous cookie (bread-bun with currants) spread thick with jam, and a glass of milk to wash it down. I still remember how delicious those cookies tasted, although stuffing our faces was probably not conducive to the energetic exercises we were about to engage in! After all the races had been run and all the games played, everyone

resorted to the school, where more tea along with sandwiches, cookies and a whole array of fancies, were provided. Then came the giving out of the prizes.

Following the day's activities, a dance was held, which went on till the early hours of the ensuing morning.

Gowking Day

I've often retold an amusing story that occurred during my childhood - of a servant-lad (then aged around fourteen) who worked at *Quoyostray*, named Ian. Fred o'*Quoyostray* decided to play a trick on Ian one *Gowking Day*. (A gowk is another name for a cuckoo, traditionally regarded as a rather foolish bird – hence *Gowking Day*, or, as it later became known, *April Fools Day*). Fred said to him, '*Ian, buoy, go doon tae Furse and ask Billo for a len (loan) o' his roond square*' (for helping form a right angle). Ian did as he was telt, and wandered doon to *Furse*. Bill quickly twigged on to Fredo's

prank, and said, '*Bouy, a'm right sorry, I lent the roond square tae How o'Langskaill jist the ither day, and avv no' gotten it back yit*'. So off up to *Langskaill* – away to the other side of Wasbister Loch - Ian trudged, in search of the required item. Here he was treated to a similar response, being told by

Howo that he had loaned the unusually-shaped square to Sando Pearson of *Vacquoy*. So onto Sando's Ian wended his weary way, by this time feeling disgruntled at all the walking he was having to do to lay hands on this darned square.

Sando, like the others before him, also quickly cottoned on to the prank being played. However, being a relative of Ian, he took pity on the poor boy, and told him there was no such thing as a roond square, and that all the others must have been playing a trick on him for *Gowking Day*!

Ian was horrified and thoroughly embarrassed that he had fallen for such a silly prank. The following year, he noted the approach of *Gowking Day* with a certain dread, but he determined to himself he would not be fooled second time round. To ensure this, he took a stock of food and clambered up to the wooden rafters of the barn at *Quoyostray*, where he remained the entire day – indeed until every thought of *Gowking Day* in the community had totally passed![29]

Weddings & Dances

Dances in those days were generally held in the community hall, which was located in Sourin. Weddings, on the other hand, were more often than not performed in the barn of the farm belonging to the bride's parents (a tradition that was soon to die out completely). Both Jean and Anna, for example, got married in *Innister*'s barn, exactly two years apart. It was a major task clearing out the barn for such a function, then cleaning the walls and floor to make it suitable for an evening's entertainment, knowing that folk

---

[29] Fred (Kirkness) o'*Quoyostray* & family later moved to Fraserburgh. Freddie was 1 of the 5 crew-members lost at sea in the Fraserburgh Lifeboat disaster of January 1970. His body was never found.

would be attired in their best outfits. Additionally, items like buckets, bushels[30] and shovels were all removed to make room for wedding guests. The wedding was held on the upper floor at *Innister*'s barn; guests entering via a ramp leading up to the sheaf-door. The stairway was boarded up so that no-one who got worse for wear with drink could fall downstairs!

My mother always baked big cakes for the occasion, while neighbours also helped with baking other items. The wedding cake itself might be baked locally or bought in from the mainland. While folk partied in the barn, there would be two or more settings in the farmhouse, when folk would come in for a sit-down meal, prepared by the bride's family and neighbours. Once these had finished eating, they would go back to the barn to dance, and another batch of guests would move into the house for a feed.

---

[30] A round wooden container with handles at the top, used to measure quantities of oats, etc. Turned the other way up, the men would stand on it to put sheaves through the mill.

Musical Entertainment

A local group of musicians usually played at such events – often it was the *'Boys o'Saviskaill'*, consisting of Stanley,

Fraser and young Edwin (who was the same age as me). Stanley and Edwin both played the accordion, while Peem o'*Tou* also joined in on the fiddle. When it came to dancing, however, no-one could beat the Mainland brothers from *Westness*. Jock and Jeemo, especially, along with their brother Rob o'*Nerse* were all terrific dancers, and were usually the first to take to the floor. Each had a similar short, broad-set frame and I well remember them dancing the night away at various Rousay dances. Boy could they dance![31]

Family Photo

During the period when one of my siblings was planning their wedding, Robert was finishing his time of service in the Army, and couldn't get home until the late summer of that year. If the wedding had been arranged for a month or two later, then all the Marwick siblings – the entire thirteen of us – would have been together under one roof at the same time - marking the first time ever that all the family would be together. But, for whatever reason, it was felt that the wedding needed to be held on the earlier date. So the

---

[31] One of the brothers, Jeemo, actually died dancing, while on the floor with my sister-in-law, Isabella at a dance in Sourin hall.

wedding went ahead as scheduled, and a terrific doo it was. Twelve siblings were together for the occasion. Poor Robert missed out, still on his way home from India. He must have felt pretty homesick that night, knowing every one of his brothers and sisters were celebrating together in his home island – and he was many hundreds of miles away on his own.

Nettie got married on the mainland parish of Harray. It was here that the family photo that has been widely circulated over the years was taken (see photo section). Indeed, it's the only extant photo that features as many as eleven of the Marwick siblings together – David and Betty being the only two not present.

Jim's New Jersey

Being a young hard-working man on the farm kept Jim very fit. Indeed, he was known to be able to run the two miles round Wasbister Loch in a record time of just ten minutes! He also served as Wester goal-keeper in inter-parish football matches. Jim was regarded as a first-class farmer, and won numerous awards in ploughing, sheep-shearing, hoeing, seed & root shows, as well as the cattle shows, all of which events were hugely popular in Rousay in my youth.

To unwind, Jim loved dancing. Indeed, he was rarely off the dance-floor at local dances. On the approach of one dance in the Sourin hall, Jim asked his mother if she would knit him a jersey to wear at the event. He didn't give her many days' notice, and she already had a hundred-and-one other chores to attend to. But she wasn't going to let him down. The task required the knitting of six body panels, as well as arms, cuffs, waistband and neckband. Then all

would have to be sewn together. But sure enough, when Friday night arrived, there was a beautiful white jumper waiting for Jim to try on. It fitted perfectly. Boy, was Jim proud of that jersey as he wore it to the dance that night. Many a person would have commented on it, and there's a fair chance he would have been eyed up by one or more eligible young females present as he danced the night away!

Popular Island Songs

When I was young classic Orkney songs like 'Lonely Scapa Flow' and 'Kirkwall Bay' hadn't even been conceived. But we had our own favourites. A popular song in Rousay was 'My Own Island Home'. I believe I first heard it from my mother, who used to sing aloud while doing the housework. I loved it, and quickly learned the words and tune by heart. I, too, would sing it out loud, and remember teaching it to both Sydney and Jean. But it's a not a song you ever hear nowadays – having been almost completely forgotten. I changed the word, 'Orkney' to 'Rousay', so as to make the song more personal.

'My Own Island Home'

There's a place on this earth,
It's the land of my birth,
A land that I'll love all my days;
And where e'er I may go,
I'll return there I know,
There's a welcome to greet me always.

Chorus
In my island home of Rousay,
It's the place that I love best;
Its beauty and grandeur are great to behold,
Its hills clothed in purple and turning to gold.
Sweet memories will linger, where e'er I may roam;
Of the Island of Rousay, my own island home.

For through dark clouds of war,
I have travelled afar,
Yet thoughts of my home e'er would be;
Of the oil lamp turned low,
And the peat burning glow,
In the croft on the hill by the sea.

In my island home of Rousay,
It's the place that I love best;
The sun sinking slowly, away in the west,
The skies ever changing, as day goes to rest;
Sweet memories will linger, where e'er I may roam;
Of the Island of Rousay, my own island home. [32]

---

[32] I remember being asked to sing this song along with my sister, Jean, at her daughter, Mary's wedding reception in Fife. To my great surprise, a non-Orcadian guest present began singing the song along with us! He

Another local song I learned in my youth was '*The Smiling Orkney Isles'*, written by Willie Kemp in the early 1930s. It's another largely forgotten composition, but it has some fine lyrics.

'The Smiling Orkney Isles'

You can sing about sunshine in far foreign lands,
Your sweet-scented woodlands or downs;
You can sing about mountains or rivers and lakes,
The prairies or streets in the town.
But give me the place of the north Scottish shore,
Where the wild surging grey-black North Sea;
Meets the rolling Atlantic those islands among,
And there is the one place for me.

Chorus:
For there's nothing but smiles in the Orkney Isles,
Where the wild rugged shores pierce the sea;
Oh what can compare to the peat-scented air,
And salt spray that rise in the breeze.
You can keep scorching sunshine in tropical lands,
But give me the red midnight sun;
Where the quaint old north dialect can only be heard,
In the Orkney Isles second to none.

To be happy is easy in these Orkney Isles,
From the north to South Ronaldsay;
You'll find it's the same from the East to the West,
From Stromness to Small Copinsay.

---

had served in Orkney during the war, and remembered hearing it several times while stationed there.

But those charming islands are all very well,
Your heart will be soon in a whirl;
Captivated you'll be by a different spell,
The charming Orcadian girls.

We also used to sing a really old song containing the *teu-neems* (nicknames) given to the inhabitants of the various islands and parishes in Orkney long ago – *'Stronsay Limpets'*, *'Wyre Whelks'*, *'Gairsay Buckies'*, *'Orphir Yirnings'*, *'Kirkwall Starlings'*, etc – there being an intriguing story behind each name. There are many verses to this delightful yet little-known song. The verse referring to my home island goes;

A 'Rousay Mare' crossed o'er the deep
Came in by the steamer, 'Bess';
And close at her heels, a 'Shapinsay Sheep'
A fact I'm ashamed to confess

Chorus: There's one more river......, (and so on)
.....I mind the tune weel.

Christmas Time

Christmas at *Innister*

No big fuss was made in Rousay about Christmas in the way that it is now. No Christmas tree, no decorations, no carol service, no week's holidays or anything of the sort. The event was celebrated simply at *Innister* - with a special roast chicken dinner (never turkey, a luxury known only to the wealthy).

There was no mountain of flashy presents either. No child got gifts from outwith the family, and few were received

from within the family either. I did usually get some small gift from Santa, but the staple present was a piece of fruit in the bottom of the stocking we hung by the fireplace on Christmas Eve. This was usually an apple or orange; never a banana (they hadn't yet been introduced on the island). But it was special to us, for it was virtually the only time of the year we ever ate a piece of fresh fruit.

Buried Bag

One year when Sydney came home at Christmas, he brought with him some presents for his youngest siblings. On Christmas morning I discovered a parcel by the fireplace. Greatly excited, I opened it to find a lovely handbag, pale blue in colour, around seven inches wide, with a flap that folded over, and the logo of a wee white poodle on the front right-hand side. I can mind it as weel as can be. I loved it, and for days carried it almost everywhere. Some days later Nettie and I fell out about something trivial (we were normally very good friends). Although Nettie won the argument, she still decided to take revenge. Sneaking up to my bedroom, she stole my treasured handbag out of the trunk. When no-one was looking, she took it outside and buried it in the large plot of earth in front of the house. I was very upset to find my beautiful bag had disappeared.

Correctly guessing it was Nettie who took it, I constantly nagged at her to get it back.

It was three full weeks before she finally relented and dug up the now rather dirty bag, returning it to its rightful owner. I cleaned the dirt off, and found to my great relief that it was none the worse for wear. Forgiving my sister (sort of) for her unkindly action, I continued to proudly carry that bag for many's a day to come.

Square o'Bannock

That same Christmas, Sydney decided to play a wee prank on Donald. He very neatly wrapped a little gift about two inches square, and attached a greeting, addressed to me. But he quite deliberately put it in Donald's stocking. He then hung it high up on the wooden pulley-dryer in the kitchen. On Christmas morning, Donald was quick to notice his stocking hanging on the dryer above him. Lowering the pulley, he grabbed the sock and excitedly dug into it, pulling out the tiny mystery gift. Wondering what it might be, he noticed to his dismay that the gift tag had my name on it. Disappointedly, he handed it over to me. I undid the wrapping and found inside a piece of bere banncok, carefully cut into a square. It

was all a big joke. I wasn't disappointed because I already had another, delightful gift from Sydney (the blue handbag). Meanwhile, on realising what was inside, Donald wasn't so cut up about it not being for him after all!

Sledging

The *Innister* bairns used to love sledging in the wintertime. Jean, Donald, Anna, Betty and myself - we all loved it, especially on a fine moon-lit night. We used to sledge down a well-sloped field between *Innister* and *Furse*. We would go out in the early evening right after our dinner and sledge to our hearts' content until we were called in at bedtime. I mind that we never seemed to get cold – the continual routine of sledging down the hill and climbing back up it again, kept us nice and warm.

New Year

Like Christmas, New Year wasn't celebrated then as it is now. I have no memory of taking in the New Year, nor of anyone first-footing. My mother always baked a large currant bun for the occasion, and the Marwicks enjoyed a special dinner together on New Year's Day - which was greatly appreciated - but there was nothing more in the way of celebrations than that. There was, however, a local custom that some of the men followed, of going out shooting for rabbits on New Year's Day, a tradition observed in some places to this day. Several of my brothers engaged in this activity. Similarly, Halloween was observed - not in the way it's done now, with 'trick or treat' or 'guising' – but simply by dooking for apples in a big tub at school, or biting into others that were hanging on strings from the ceiling.

Working on the Farm

Harvest Work

The harvest in those days involved a lot of work. The hay was cut by a reaper, but everything else was done by hand, such as gathering the crop together to form sheaves, then tying the sheaves together using a band made by a stretch of loose straw. There was a real knack to making the bands, but all of us youngsters at *Innister* soon learned it, and before long were masters of the craft. The sheaves were then of course stacked into stooks, each consisting of six sheaves. The amount of work involved can only be imagined by an awareness of how large the fields were, and knowing that there was field after field to work on.

Perfectionist Family

The Marwicks were known throughout Wester and beyond to be perfectionists when it came to their farm work. Everything had to be 'just right'. This was a trait my brothers inherited from their father, who was very particular in all he did. None of his sons owned that perfectionist trait more than Jim. I remember that when gathering the oats together to make sheaves, which I used to help with, Jim would come along behind me and point out every last strand of oat that I had overlooked, insisting I picked it up. *'You've missed some strands o'stray!'* he would shout.

Jim was equally scrupulous when it came to sowing oat-seeds, which was done by throwing handfuls of seed onto the ploughed field - one to the right-hand side, the other to the left – from the happer, a large open bowl which was attached by strap and worn over the shoulder, while secured also around the waist. I used to come to him with buckets of seed to pour into the happer. Naturally some would miss and fall to the ground. I would instantly stand on these loose seeds and bury them into the ground, to hide them from Jim's searching eyes! If he ever saw me spilling seeds, he would invariably make me stoop down and pick up the free-fall.

Another of Jim's fixations became apparent when separating turnip plants. Each plant had to be an exact distance from the next, and he was very quick to point out if I, or another family member, had made them too close together or too far apart. Such negligence had to be corrected. Jim's eye for absolute detail in all these matters irritated me no end when I was doing my best to help out, but at the same time I deeply appreciated how hard my older brother worked on the farm, and I quietly admired his desire that everything be done with such spirit of excellence.

All Fall Down

I would also help out at building loads of hay at *Innister* during the harvest-time. The farm owned a large, wide, flat sleigh, which was built on runners. In the field, I would stand on the sleigh and build the load, as Roderick forked up sheaves to me, also helping me keep the load square. The farm horse would pull the sleigh in towards the site where the haystack was being built. Stack-building was a real art, and was usually performed by Jim, who formed them so beautifully.

As a full sleigh was being brought in one evening, I was lying on top of the high load of sheaves they had carted from the field. Maybe the load was too big, or for some other reason, the load began to fall apart, and I came tumbling down from my lofty position. Luckily, I fell onto sheaves of hay that had fallen before me, so I got a fairly soft landing,

and wasn't hurt. But my pride was, all the more because Roderick was standing by the way enjoying a good laugh at my expense. He was quick to tell me he had never seen me move so fast in his life! No-one got blamed for the incident – we just stuck in and built the load again. I built many a load like that each harvest-time.

After the harvest had been taken in, it was customary to put one or two hen-houses – which had been very ably built by Roderick when he was just in his mid-teens - into the fields so that the hens could feast off the freshly harvested fields. During the summer the hen-houses were situated on the hill-slope above the farm. Each day someone would make up hen-food (*'Layers Mash'* meal, mixed with tatties unfit for human consumption, boiled in large pots), mix it with water, and carry it in two buckets up to the hens at *Knock-ha'* – a fair weight to carry such a distance each day.

Making Sookans

After the stack was built we would make sookans to hold it down against the strong winds that regularly hit Rousay in the winter. A sookan was a type of rope, only it was made completely out of straw. Its formation was a truly skilled operation. Loose strands of stray were fed into a kraa-kruik – a metal tool with a ratchet handle, made for the purpose – which twisted the strands of stray very tightly together. As I worked the kruik, which I often did, I stepped further and further away from my brother, who was continually feeding straw

into it. In this way the sookan got longer and longer and eventually great lengths of thick stray-rope could be made, which were tied in a tight knot at the ends to keep their shape.

We used to spend entire mornings engaged in this activity – two or four of us working together. We had three kruiks on the farm, so they could be used simultaneously. It was very tiring work when doing it for hours on end – and we never broke off for a cup of tea the way folk do now. But eventually we would fashion several lengths of sturdy straw-rope which would get used to tie down a stack of sheaves, or to secure a net thrown over a stack of loose hay.

Bed-Sacks

The kruiks were stored away during the winter, but during the summer and autumn when in use, they were hung on hooks at the end of the fanners. This was a device through which sheaves of oats were passed to remove the chaff – the light, leaf-like coating around the oats. The pure oats were used to bake or cook with, or as seed to sow for the following year. The chaff was used as kye-bedding in the byre during winter.

But it wasn't just used for the kye's bedding – but for ours too! Well do I mind my mother going into the chaffy-hoose – part of the mill – and pulling out lots of chaff. This we stuffed into a strong, striped sacking material known as *'ticking'* to make nice, cosy mattresses. Not that we ever called them by that fancy name – they were simply 'bed-sacks'. The bed-sacks were filled with fresh chaff every year. At all times, but especially when newly filled, you just sank into them when you went to bed at night – they really were right comfy.

Threshing

Well do I mind having to go out in the dark at various points through the winter and help the men thresh (separate the oats from the stray) by light from the paraffin lamp. Threshing was done in the mill – situated upstairs in the barn and separated from the granary by a partition. Sheaves were taken by cart from the stack to the big sheaf door at the barn, and thrown inside, where they had to be carefully arranged, as normally a whole stack of sheaves would be taken in at one time. I would throw the sheaves up on a sheaf-board one by one, from where one of my brothers would feed them into the vast, noisy threshing machine. We always watched out for small stones or chunks of dried mud stuck to the sheaves – any we missed would rattle menacingly in the mill, and occasionally even spin out and hit someone in the face.

The stray went downstairs via a big hatch located by the thresher, and the oats via a small chute, and straight into a sack hooked onto the end of it, which required to be routinely changed once full. The stray was packed away at the far end of the barn, and used to feed the kye over the winter months. There was a lot of work involved in threshing, yet it was always regarded as an add-on to the day's activities – performed late in the evening after the rest of the day's work was done.

The steep Leean, reputedly the highest road in Orkney. Wester school is lower-left, & across from it, Cogar & Ivybank. Beyond the school is Langskaill farm.

Wasbister from the Leean. Innister is located towards the upper right.

The Loch o'Wasbister and Burrian Isle, a crannog – artificial island - used as a settlement during the Iron Age.

Grinding the Meal

Innister owned a huge girnal, which was kept in the granary, located at the end of the barn. It consisted of a big box-like structure at each end, with a division in the middle. One end was for oatmeal; the other end for bere-meal.[33] We had no porridge oats in those days.

After the harvest was finished each year, it was taken at various times by horse and cart to Sourin Mill, where it was ground into oat and bere-meal, before being packed into bags. My brothers would take their dinner early on those days, so they could set off to the Mill, get the flour ground, and return home by evening.

From quite an early age one of my sisters and I used to go into the girnal and tramp down the bere and oat meal so that the container could hold even more; indeed, enough to last our family through the winter. It was hard work, but we found it great fun. The oatmeal was used to make porridge and oatcakes; the bere was used to make bere-bannocks. We

---

[33] A creamy coloured whole flour made from an especially pure variety of barley, which has been grown in Orkney for centuries.

packed the meal with our bare feet (making sure our feet were reasonably clean, of course, as the family would be eating the meal).

Scrubbing the Girnal

The walls of the girnal had to be scrubbed down annually, otherwise they might get mited with the meal sticking to it. I remember one occasion when Jean and I were told to perform this task. We climbed over some boxes to get into the girnal. Then we scrubbed away like goodo, but only when we had finished did we consider how we were going to get out of the huge container, which was of course empty at the time, and had quite high sides. I was tall; Jean, on the other hand, was fairly short and a bit stockier. We were also both very young. I managed to somehow clamber out. Realising the sides of the girnal were way above her own meagre height, Jean struggled to climb out. '*Help, Help!* she cried several times, her voice echoing through the empty chamber. I found the incident highly amusing, and could only stand back and laugh out loud as Jean stood alone helpless in that vast empty box. Eventually I came to my sister's aid, and she was able to clamber out. We walked back to the farmhouse together, Jean hardly knowing whether to thank me or wallop me!

Knarston, in the Sourin district, where my father's family came from. The island beyond is Egilsay, and beyond that, Eday.

The former general store and Post Office (to the right) at Hullion in Frotoft, where my mother was born and raised. In earlier years, the veritable township of Hullion also comprised a farm, mill, bakery & drapers business.

Innister from the main road. The hill-slope beyond is Knock'ha.

The striking view afforded from Knock'ha, showing Innister and Wasbister Loch, with the Bay o'Saviskaill and Keirfea Hill in the distance.

The ruins o' Moan, with Keirfea & the Head of Farraclett in the distance.

3 rows of Wester dwellings. In the foreground, the ruins of Quoys. Behind is Quoyostray, & to the right, Quoygray & Kevady (& beyond, the ruins of Breckan). To the rear left sits Hammerfield, Lower Hammerfield & Tou.

The Lobust, a massive stack of rock off the north-west coast of Rousay.

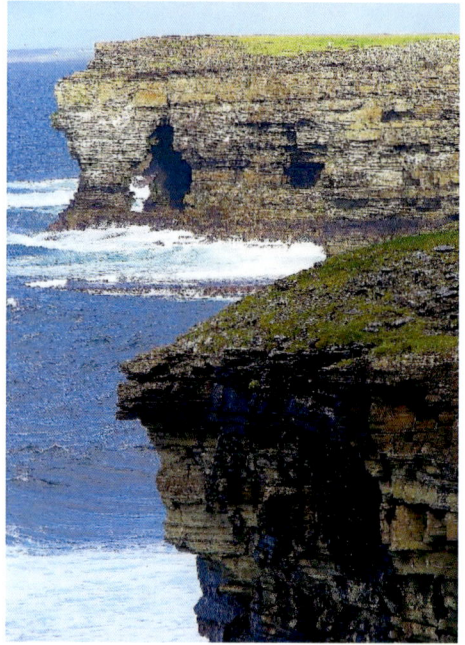

2 natural arches in the cliffs at Sacquoy Head.

Near the Lobust, one of Rousay's numerous dramatic geos.

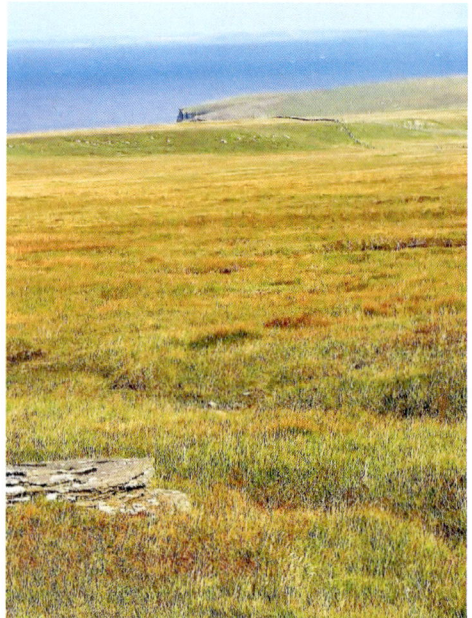

The vast wilderness between Innister & the shore, known as the Brings.

Fertile fields on Rousay's westside. Midhowe Broch & Cairn nestle by the shore. Eynhallow rises in the glimmering Sound, & beyond, the mainland parish of Evie.

Brigsend (right), near Westness. Across the road is Duke Street (ruins), plus a long track leading up the hills to Muckle Water, by far Rousay's largest loch.

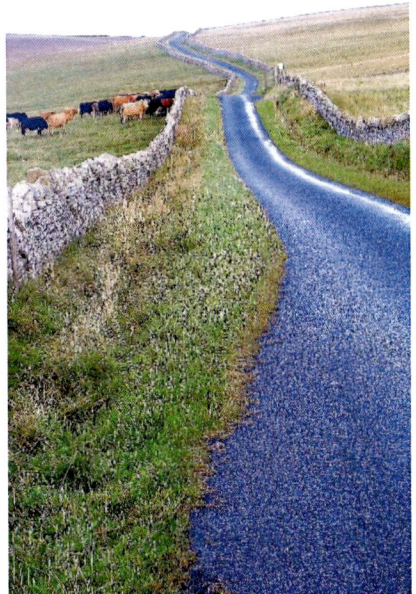

Well-crafted stone dykes line the twisted road through Quandal, now inhabited only by cattle & sheep.

Looking down on Swartifield & the Head of Farraclett. Beyond, left you can just make out Westray, & to the right the islands of Faray and Eday.

Foreground, the stepped braes above Swartifield, where I played as a child. Fa'Doun sits under the brae. To the left is Brinian, & the isle of Wyre beyond.

The stepped braes showing prominently on the steep slopes below the Leean, looking towards Wasbister in the distance.

Sourin Kirk (now a ruin) which I used to attend with my aunt. The manse can be seen beyond the church.

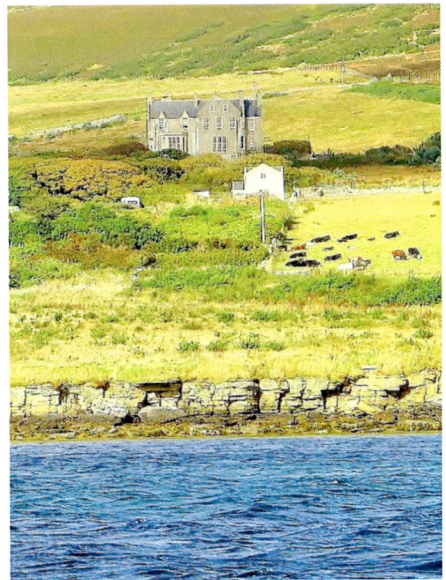

The stately Trumland House in Brinian, commissioned by F. W. Traill-Burroughs in 1870 as a family home following his return from India.

Panoramic view of Wasbister from high on the Wester hills. In the centre sits Wasbister Loch, surrounded by the farms of Saviskaill, Sketquoy & Fealquoy. The island beyond is Westray, with the sheer cliffs of Noup Head to the left.

Left and above: Laying flowers at the graveside of my parents at Wasbister cemetery, located by the shores of Wester Loch, August 2017. My brothers, Jim & Roderick, & their wives, are also buried here.

The 3 surviving Marwick sisters on my 80th birthday. From left; Nettie, me, Anna. Sadly, Anna passed away ten months later (photo courtesy of Fiona

Holding my most recent great-grandchild, just a few weeks old, on my 90th birthday.

With time to reflect while enjoying a cuppa, summer 2017.

In my 90th year, while on holiday in Edinburgh.

Herding the Kye

I loved herding the kye when I was young. *Innister* owned a big black dog called *Peter*, which I was extremely fond of, and he was always with me when I herded the kye (a sizeable herd of around thirty). I performed this duty every summer from the age of nine and upwards. The kye had to be taken from the braes o' *Knock-ha'* down to the byre in the morning, where they were individually tied up and milked, a time-consuming task. Then I would herd them down to the field where they were to graze for the rest of the morning. They were accorded a particular narrow strip of grass each summer's day, stretching out along the length of the field. My job was to watch over them, making sure they didn't stray outwith the allotted strip of land. I really didn't have to do much, for *Peter* went after any stray coo without even being told, bringing it back into the fold. He seemed to

know by pure instinct the unmarked boundaries beyond which they were not to cross. Even *Peter* had little work to do – he would just creep along behind any straying coo, and it would immediately move back. I took my knitting needles and some wool with me and would while away the day knitting, standing all the time. I thoroughly enjoyed the whole experience, loving being outdoors on these long summer days when Wester glowed with beauty.

In the afternoon, the kye were taken back to the braes o' *Knock-ha'* – through the gate at the end of the field, and in to the wide open grazing land for the remainder of the day. They were then taken back to the byre again in the early evening for milking, before being again returned to *Knock-ha'* overnight. The whole process was repeated the following day, and the next, throughout the long summer.

Calving

There were two byres at *Innister* – a milkers byre and the stirks byre (stirks were half-grown kye, between six and twelve months old – for no particular reason we called them *'stricks'*). My sisters and I were never allowed in the byre when a cow was calving – indeed I have never seen a calf being born to this day. Not that there was any ban on me entering the byre on other occasions of course. Indeed, I was required to go in on an almost daily basis, to feed the kye, to milk them, to feed the calves, and so on.

Ploughing

I had a great laugh with my brother, Jim one day when he was out ploughing a field below the farm. The plough was pulled by the farm horse, *Prince*, who, from long experience, well understood Jim's single-word commands. They were approaching the end of a drill at one point, so Jim shouted 'Woa', and *Prince* stopped at once. Realising they had come to a halt a little prematurely, Jim ordered, '*A peedie bit yit*'! I was standing nearby, and quickly ran behind a stack and had a hearty laugh at the thought of Jim expecting *Prince*, smart though he was, to understand an order like that (though it's quite possible he actually did!) Thankfully Jim, on hearing my laughter from the other side of the stack, was able to see the funny side of it, too (while *Prince* probably looked on wondering what droll creatures humans were).

Neepie Wark

An enormous amount of work was involved in growing turnips in my young days, and a considerable assortment of both horse-drawn and hand-tools was required in the long-drawn-out process, such as a turnip sower, a scarifier, a scuffler, and of course, long-handled hoes. These were used for thinning the plants when they grew to be a few inches high. This monotonous task alone involved participation from most members of the family and took a good number of days to complete.

Innister had its own neep-shed, which was located between the two byres. It had a huge door, to allow the entry of a cart full of neeps after they had been picked from the field. A neep-chapper was kept in the shed, common to most farms in those days. During the winter time, neeps were chopped and thrown to the kye in the byres. Three of us were normally involved in this activity. I would grab a neep and put it in the chapper; one of my sisters would chap it, ie, pull down a heavy arm which would cut the neep into thick slices. Then one of our brothers - often Donald - would collect the sliced neeps into a big wire basket - *'the neepie basket'* - and go and throw them to the kye. This served as deserved treat for them in the winter, when they were tied up in the byre for months on end.

Swedes

But it wasn't just as a treat that neeps were given to the kye. They acted as a form of laxative and were also high in protein. (In distinction, the farm horses were only given swedes – I never knew the reason for this. *Innister* grew both neeps (or *'yellows'*, because they had a yellowy skin), and to a lesser extent, swedes (purple at the top) – both grown in separate drills in the same field. Only swedes were brought into the house for cooking – we never ate neeps, which had a bitter taste. Swedes, on the other hand, the Marwicks adored, not least when mashed with boiled tatties and served with a chunk of butter, to form Orkney's traditional dish, and an all-round favourite at *Innister* - clapshot. At home we loved clapshot most when served with minced beef - you really can't beat mince and clapshot! - or with *Princes* corned beef – another favourite combination.

Up in the Peat-Hill

Hard Day's Work

Almost every home on Rousay used peats as a source of home-fuel – it was, after all free energy. But it was only free in one sense. The amount of work involved was colossal. This included at varying stages, *'flaying'* the banks (cutting off the heathery turf); digging the peats with a *'tusker'* (a long wooden-handled tool with a sharp angled blade); spreading them flat on the ground to dry and stiffen; setting them upright in threes or fours to dry fully (for up to several weeks); grouping them in larger *'roos'* at the edge of the bank for uplifting; stacking them onto a cart, carting them home, and building them carefully into a peat-stack. From start to finish the whole process could last several months.

The Marwicks cut their peats high up in the Wester hills, on the western slopes of *Keirfea*, well beyond *White Meadows*. You got there by turning right at *Langskaill*, and following a long, narrow dirt track along the face of the hillside. I used to regularly walk the long distance from *Innister* up to the peat hill, sometimes with one of my sisters but often on my own, and do a good day's labour, before trudging all the way back home again to prepare dinner for the family (I often made soup, followed by salt herring, chicken or stew). After clearing the dishes, I would then have to go out and milk the kye and perform other farm duties. It made for a long, hard day's work.

All the men from the various farmsteads would come together to help with each family's peats. *Langskaill, Sketquoy,* and many other farmsteads cut their peats in the same hill, though some had their peat-banks nearer to home, eg in the peaty area above *Everybist.* As we passed by *White Meadows* on the way to the peatbanks, Lizzie would always be out to greet us. Living so far removed from any other Rousay dwelling, she had fewer opportunities of socialising with other Wester folk. So on the rare occasion of someone passing their house, she was keen to come out for a blether.

Pear Juice

Some days, when *Innister's* men were at work in the peats, Anna would drive the farm's horse-and-cart up to the banks, laden with dinner for all the men. This included soup, a meat course and a pudding! My mother believed her boys deserved hearty nourishment when they were working so hard. The cooked dinners were carefully packed with a thick cushion of hay from the haystack to keep them warm.

On one occasion when I accompanied Anna to the hill, desert consisted of custard, served with pears from a large tin bought from the grocer-van. This was a rare treat in Rousay in those days. Jim was in charge of dishing out the dinner to each worker. After the first two courses had been

consumed, I handed Jim the huge tin of pears. He opened it, and served out helpings of fruit and custard to all the men present. But, lovingly, he kept back some juice in the tin, which he handed back to me, for my own consumption. I had never tasted pear juice before, and boy did I enjoy that delicious drink, especially on that warm summer's day. What a treat! Jim was so good to me.

Brewing Ale

But it wasn't only food that my mother provided for her peat-cutting family. A great many homes in Rousay brewed in those days. Though not a drinker herself, my mother brewed once a year – always at the time of the annual peat-cutting season. A good dozen or more bottles of ale would be packed in straw and taken up to the peat-hill for the men. A much anticipated reward for the genuinely hard work they put into the peat-cutting process.

Yet, much as the Marwicks loved their hard-earned ale, I virtually never mind any of my brothers drinking at home. Alcohol was only consumed on significant social occasions; for example at a wedding, or a dance in Sourin hall (for which event a half-bottle of whisky might even occasionally be purchased).

Other Farm Activities

Wool

Each year, after the sheep were clipped in the summer, my mother would send all the fleece off to the world-famous *Hunters of Brora* woollen mill in Sutherland, where it was

spun into wool. This would then be sent back to *Innister*. Some of it might be sold to *Shearers* in Kirkwall, while some was sent to another firm to make blankets, for use on some of the innumerable *Innister* beds!

Over a period of several years Betty and I, being the only two girls staying on the farm at that time, were allowed a fleece each of us. This constituted a lot of wool. We would thoughtfully choose wool-quantities of different colours, each amount enough to knit a garment of our choosing, any size we wanted. When the wool arrived back home, we would pick out our own portions, which we would then proceed to knit into our desired garments. This was a great delight to both of us increasingly fashion-conscious girls!

The Well

Throughout my twenty years in Rousay, water had to be transported to the farmhouse by hand, there being no running water anywhere on the premises. Either myself or one of my sisters would go to the well at the dam and carry two bucket-fulls of water back to the farm. This was a twice-daily routine, and I performed the task hundreds of times. Consisting of cool spring water, it made for a truly refreshing drink. The transported water was also used for making tea, for personal hygiene purposes and for washing dishes, etc.

Water Water Everywhere

During the occasion of the birth of Jim and Isabella's son, Alistair, I had to go and fetch six buckets of water from the well, as there was no water in the house. Three times I went, carrying back two bucket-fulls each time. There was a large flag-stone lying between the byre and *Innister*'s porch door (I can remember the exact size and shape of it). One corner of the flag-stone stuck up a peedie bit, and on my second trip home from the well, I tripped on this projected edge. Down I fell, flat on my face, not being able to soften my fall with my arms because both hands were holding buckets of water.

The contents of these now spilled everywhere, not least all over me! I was bruised, hurt, soaked, and thoroughly shaken by the sudden fall – but one of my siblings, who saw it all happening from the porch door, found the incident hilarious, and laughed himself silly, perhaps not realising how shaken I was. In fact, after drying off, and tending my cuts and bruises, I had to go upstairs to bed for an hour to recover from the incident. Yet, when I eventually got up, I still had to go and fetch the final two buckets of water from the well – nobody had shown sufficient sympathy to go and do it for me!

Washing Klaes

Of course all the clothes had to be washed by hand in those days. This we did in a big wooden tub – literally a half-barrel, located up in the auld hoose. I mind washing the klaes many's a time – and hard work it was. To begin with, we had to go and fetch the water. We didn't use water from the well for this, which was considered too 'hard'. Instead we used water from the dam, which was softer, and better

for washing clothes. We would coup the water up in our buckets, always using an area at the side of the dam which the kye didn't use when they went for a drink.

It seems odd now, but we didn't have such a thing as a clothes-line in those days, so after getting washed, the klaes were simply hung over a fence to get dried. It was a blooming nuisance picking the dried clothes off the fence, as they would stick to the barbed wire. Towels were spread out on the green on a fine day, to hopefully get bleached by the sun, should it decide to make an appearance.

Bartering with Eggs

The surplus eggs not required at *Innister*, my mother used to take down to the horse-drawn grocer van that passed by the end of the farm road each week, where they were used as barter for groceries. All farms did the same thing. The extra money earned would be paid in cash. The eggs would be carefully placed on cardboard egg-trays, and packed into one of two large baskets, which had handles fitted on the top. Every week, I, or one of my sisters would assist my mother in carrying these huge baskets all the way down to the van. Of course they had to be transported carefully so that none of the eggs broke. The grocer would remove the trays of eggs and place them onto boxes that lined one side of his van – each box would hold as many as thirty dozen eggs. I often wondered if he truly managed to transport this vast quantity of eggs up the rough, steep *Leean* road, and back to Sourin, by horse and rattly cart, without breaking any. I bet he didn't!

Rabbits

Many men on Rousay caught rabbits on their farms or in the hills and sold them to dealers outwith the island. Among the Marwicks, Donald was one who caught a lot of rabbits; as did both Johnny and Roderick. They were then gutted, but were left unwashed, as this allowed the meat to stay fresher for longer. Next the rabbits were packed into sacks, which were then sewn up and taken for posting. Even at the Post Office, blood would seep out of the sacks and drip onto the floor. One company that bought the rabbits was *Agnews* of Glasgow. Another popular firm was based in Leeds. I recall one man being asked, *'Where do you send your rabbits to – to Leeds?'* *'Oh, no'*, replied the man, *'some place in England!'* The sacks would no doubt have been sent second class to save money. I've often wondered what condition those rabbits would arrive way down in South Yorkshire in, several long days after being posted – surely they couldn't have been very appetising for anyone to eat!

Eating to Live

Butter

After the kye were milked (twice a day), a portion of the milk was kept aside for drinking. The rest of it had to be separated (skimmed); the separator then having to be cleaned on a daily basis. The separated milk was used to feed the calves. Cream from the milk was used to make butter. The cream had to be kirned in the churn - a task that was done once a week after a healthy build-up of cream had formed.

The kirning produced a mass lump of butter. We used a butter-spoon (which wasn't in a spoon-shape at all, but had a flat, ribbed edge), which we worked into the butter, cutting it into large oblong chunks for use at mealtimes. All the butter made at *Innister* was used on the farm – none was sold. It was lovely and creamy – I've never since tasted butter quite like it.

The residue – the kirned milk, was used mainly for baking, although it was also quite delicious to drink. I always preferred it when two or three days old, by which time it was already going 'sharp' – this I found a great thirst-quencher (though I couldn't drink it like that now!). I mind some of my brothers used to add oatmeal to a bucket of kirned milk, stir it, then dip an enamel mug into it for a cool, nourishing snack.

Spilt Milk

During my childhood the local nurse in Rousay - Nurse Park - went back to her home community on mainland Scotland to get married. Arriving back in Rousay, a reception was held in the Sourin Hall for all her island friends. Almost all the Marwicks were invited. I remember walking home from the dance as late as seven o'clock the following morning after a great evening's partying! I arrived home, shattered from the night's entertainment and the long walk home. But instead of going to bed, which is what

I really wanted to do, I decided that since it was already early morning, I would kirn the cream.

Having changed into my ordinary clothes, I went into the dairy, unclipped the lid on the side of the kirn, poured the bucket of thick cream into it, and clipped the lid back on securely, as I had done many times before. At least, I *thought* I had secured the lid firmly. But as soon as I began to turn the handle to churn the cream, it all came gushing out and onto the dairy floor, splashing everywhere. A whole week's cream lost in a few seconds. What a mess! I wished I had gone straight to bed as soon as I got home – and left the kirning till I was more awake and alert.

Now I had the arduous task of cleaning the rich, greasy cream off the dairy floor and everywhere else it had splashed onto – a time-consuming task for a totally exhausted young woman who was, all the while, feeling rather the worse for wear!

Catching Cuithes

One advantage of living in a rural island location was that there was an abundance of natural resources. Like everyone else, the folk at *Innister* took advantage of this as much as possible. My brothers often went to the cliffs at the back of *Sketquoy* to fish for cuithes,[34] which would make a very tasty dinner the following day, when fried in butter. The boys would fish by line from part-way down the cliffs – quite a

---

[34] Coalfish, aged between one and two years. Younger and older coalfish were known as sillocks and saithe, respectively.

dangerous venture, requiring plenty of skill and agility. Anna and I used to try and join in the fishing, and while Anna was able to climb up and down the cliffs with remarkable ease, fishing line in hand (she could virtually run up and down those cliffs), I would take tentative steps down one or two rock edges, before quickly clambering back up again! It simply wasn't for me. The cliffs were too rugged, high, and steep. Instead, I would sit on the rocks for up to two hours and wait for Anna to surface above the cliff edge, hopefully with a healthy catch of cuithes in hand. The Marwicks sometimes caught so many that it would be a fair weight just carrying them home. We would split the fish, and sundry them by laying them out on the porch-roof, or hanging them on a string along the side of the house. Once dried, they were stored away and cooked for dinner throughout the winter.

Whelks

My brothers also used to come home with buckets of shellfish they had picked from the shore. I used to sit with my siblings on the dyke at the *bigging* and eat the whelks as soon as they were boiled, drawing them out of their shells with a darning needle. I loved them, especially when eaten -- as my family always did - with bere-bannocks. But I went completely off whelks in later years, and I still don't relish the taste of them now.

Cod and Herring

We also ate a lot of cod – usually bought in packs from the van. They were as hard as boards when purchased, and having previously been dozed with salt for preservation, the water they were boiled in had to be changed several times when cooking, to reduce to palatable levels the saltiness of the fish. My mother also bought in a half-barrel of herring in the autumn. Unlike the cod, this came in a brine solution.

Although I loved fish, we ate it so often at *Innister* that some of the family got scunnered of it in later years. I got especially tired of eating cuithes, but at a later point began to enjoy fish again. Jean hardly ever ate fish again after moving away from home.

Poultry

Because the Marwicks kept hens, chicken was often served for dinner. A member of the family would have to go and kill the bird – this was done right on the spot, wherever the hen was caught. Customarily, it was one of the women who performed this unsavoury task (the men only helped out if the female was struggling). I did it many's a time. The hen was killed by holding it by its legs and traa-ing its neck – literally pulling its head off. Not a job I relished – and obviously much less pleasant for the chicken! But I became so accustomed to it that it stopped bothering me. Older poultry were the hardest to traa, because their necks were thicker. Younger chickens were much easier.

The hen was then taken into the barn and immediately plucked over a metal tub – much easier to do when the bird was still warm. It was time-consuming, but, again, I soon became accustomed to it. Younger chickens weren't plucked – they could be skinned by simply pulling the supple skin off.

Pickled Eggs

My mother often pickled eggs, especially during the wartime, placing them in a large bath filled with a vinegar solution. The bath would stand in the dairy, and eggs were taken into the house as and when required. This stock would last the family through the long winter months, when not so many eggs were being laid. I remember that the pickled eggs tasted just as fresh as if they had been laid that same day – although, to be honest, it's not a very appealing thought to me now.

Pork

The killing of the farm pig was a big event at *Innister*. The grisly operation was performed by two of the men - by slitting its throat with a knife. I remember as a young child being strictly kept indoors while this feat was carried out, so that we couldn't hear the squeals of the suffering animal, or see the bloody mess that resulted. Once killed, the pig was then gutted.

My mother used to carry the pigs guts – in two heavy buckets – down to the burn at the knowe o'*Hammer*. Here she would stand in the cold burn for up to two hours, carefully washing the entrails out, moving up the burn every now and then to get fresh water.

The meat from the pig was cleaned by dipping it into a large pot of boiling water. Then it was placed into a half-barrel of salt, which soon dissolved into a strong brine solution. The pork was stored in the auld hoose for use throughout the winter.

The Grocer Van

As you can tell, we were a fairly self-sufficient farm, and we never went hungry. We were very fortunate in that there was always food on the table. Because most of our food was home-produced, there wasn't an awful lot we needed to buy from the van when it came round Wester each week. Two food items that we did regularly buy in were beef and bread.

In any case, the van sold not only food, but also other household products, as well as paraffin from huge two-gallon cans that were stacked on racks along the outside of the van. Nearly all homes bought paraffin for their house and farm-lamps. Hygiene was a word rarely, if ever, used in those days. It was by no means uncommon for the van-man to pour out some paraffin one minute, then handle a loaf of bread or cut a pound of mince the next, without the slightest thought (or availability) of washing his hands between jobs. To be honest, nobody thought anything of it.

Furthermore, the Co-op van came round on a Tuesday afternoon, carrying unrefrigerated meat that had come across from the mainland on Monday morning (the van from the *Hullion* shop came round on Thursdays). By the time the meat got to Wester it was, to say the least, less than fresh. Besides, being located at the back end of the island, the only cuts on offer to us were those that everyone else had rejected! It never looked very appetising, but it was all there was, so we bought it, cooked it and ate it, and no-one in the family ever complained.

For all the wonderful baking my mother produced, she didn't bake bread itself. This was always bought from the van. She also bought in long fruit-loaves, several at a time; square-shaped at the ends. They invariably got scoffed in next to no time, for all the Marwicks loved them.

Sweet foods like cakes and biscuits were never purchased, and coffee wasn't heard tell of in those days. Only the truly wealthy consumed this exotic drink. After first tasting it years later, it took a long time for me to acquire a taste for it. To this day I prefer a nicely-brewed cup of tea!

Baking and Cooking

Baking

Until my sisters and I were old enough to engage in the task, baking was an almost daily chore for my mother. And it wasn't always straight forward. First she had to go out to the barn, and climb upstairs to the granary, where the girnal was located. Here she would get the meal and take it back into the kitchen to bake with. Only then could the actual baking begin. My mother was an excellent baker.

Family favourites included bere bannocks, floury bannocks and oatcakes – all placed on the iron yetlin[35], and baked on top of the stove. Another favourite at *Innister* was *'puffies'* – an oven-scone mixture set in a big lump on a baking tray and cooked in the oven. These were delicious when eaten warm and dozed with a thick layer of my mother's home-made rhubarb jam. She made stacks and stacks of rhubarb jam every year – it was the only jam the family ever got, but boy, it was right good! I can taste it still.

Taking from my mother, I developed over time into a well-seasoned baker. Indeed, when I reached my early-to-mid teens, I would bake virtually every day. My offerings were almost always well received by hard-working members of the family. Once, however, Roderick complained that that day's bere bannocks were as tough as leather half-soles, and not fit to eat! This, however, was a rare complaint.

---

[35] An old-fashioned iron griddle with a handle arched over the top. There was room for around three bannocks on the yetlin.

Clootie Dumplings

It was traditional practise that, once the harvest was finished, the women of a farm would bake a huge plum duff – or clootie dumpling as we called them - for all the men folk, as a reward for their hard work in the harvest. My mother was exceptionally good at making these. A similar cake mixture was used as for a currant bun – with lots of (dried) fruit - except that a currant bun is baked in the oven; a clootie dumpling is boiled. The ingredients were never measured out – amounts were just guessed at. My mother would always sew a cloth together – a time-consuming task in itself (some folk used an old clean pillow-case). She would soak the bag in boiling water, and wring it out as best she could. Then she turned the bag inside out, and gave it a good coating of flour on the interior side. She would then pack the baking mixture into a large lump and spoon it inside the cloth bag. This would then be placed in a huge pot, and the top tied – leaving room for expansion, but not too much, or it might fill with water. The cake was boiled for hours. Made this way, it would, at least in theory, slide easily out of the bag onto a large ashette. With the coating of flour, my mother's clootie dumplings looked really bonny, and they tasted so very good – whether eaten hot or cold. I have always sought to make my clootie dumplings exactly the same way.

Mealie Puddings

Following the killing and gutting of the farm pig, my mother would take the freshly-washed lining of the pigs stomach indoors. She would mix together some oatmeal, onions, salt and fat, and pack it all into the skin. This was then cooked into beautiful big mealie puddings. What a feast that was, served hot or cold! Vastly superior to any white pudding you could buy in a shop today, anywhere. Mum often stuck a piece of cold mealie pudding into our piece to eat at school. What a treat that was to a hungry, appreciative child. I absolutely loved it!

Chicken & Pork

After gutting and washing it thoroughly, my mum often boiled a freshly killed chicken, then fried it in her home-made butter, and served it for dinner with new tatties. Boy was that good!

Meat from the pork belly or the back of the pig was usually cut into thick slices – much thicker than a slice of today's bacon, though not quite as thick as a pork chop. My mother would fry these, and one slice, served with tatties and perhaps one other veg, was enough to make a fine, filling meal. Delicious? I've never since tasted bacon even remotely as good!

Tattie Pie

On occasions when my mother didn't have enough meat to make dinner with, she would resort to cooking tattie pie – a vast hot-pot made with whole peeled tatties, along with chunks of neep (swede), and any other vegetable as was available, such as cabbage, carrots or onions. All this was cooked in a huge pot on the stove. But what made the dish a real speciality were the beautiful dumplings (dough boys) that my mother made. These she steamed by placing on top of the vegetables, and the whole thing left to stew for a good forty minutes, or until the men came in from their morning's work. By this time the dough-boys would have risen greatly, filling the huge pot they were being cooked in. The gravy was made in the same pot: this would thicken naturally with flour that fell away from the doughboys. Served steaming hot to a family of hungry Marwicks, boy, was it good! Try as I have, I've never been able to make dumplings that were anything like as tasty.

Living at *Swartifield*

Great-Aunt Jessie

My father had an aunt, just thirteen years older than himself, called Janet Gibson (sometimes called Tess, though far more commonly, Jessie). She lived at *Swartifield*, at the Sourin end of the *Leean*. Jessie was a younger sister of Betsy, who was my father's mother and my grandmother. I never knew my grandmother, because sadly she died just after giving birth to my father. But I do remember her other sister, Isabella (Izo), who

died when I was five. Izo was short and of medium build, whereas Jessie was tall and slim.

Anna, Robert, Jean and myself used to take turns at going to stay with aunt Jessie for an overall total of nine or ten years. The idea was simply to provide company to her, for she lived alone. *Swartifield* consisted of a small but 'n' ben, with an old byre attached, although Jessie had no livestock, other than a few hens that she kept in the back-most of two wee outhouses.

Jessie worked hard in her younger days at various Sourin farms, including *Knarston*, *Scockness* and *Faraclett*; singling neeps, helping in the harvest, etc. She didn't get paid much for these jobs, and never had a lot of money about her. But she was known for her generosity, and although she lived simply, I, for one, was never left wanting during the time I stayed with her.

Jessie used to come to *Innister* for a week at a time, to help get the seed tatties ready; collecting together healthy small tatties of similar size, so they could be used to grow to maturity; meanwhile discarding any that were in any way bad. She worked her way through sack after sack of tatties in this manner each year.

Jessie was a very social character, and often visited her friends and neighbours. This may have been partly out of a sense of loneliness, as she never married. I stayed with her for nearly three years, from the age of twelve to fourteen, during some of which time I attended the Sourin school, because it was nearer to *Swartifield* than the Wester school.

The Lonely *Leean*

For many months, however, until I was age to attend the Sourin school, I continued to trudge the whole length of the long and lonely *Leean* road each morning to attend the Wester school. I'd walk back up it and down the stepped brae to *Swartifield* each afternoon after classes. I walked alone both ways. Rarely did I meet someone walking, and even more rarely a vehicle going in either direction – there being few cars on Rousay at the time. This long walk I had to take in all weathers, though I don't ever remember it snowing, nor, surprisingly do I ever recall getting a right soaking (though I almost certainly must have on numerous occasions). In any case, it probably wasn't an awful lot longer than the walk I subsequently had to make each day to the Sourin school, which was also a fair distance from *Swartifield*.

There were two steps built into the dyke by the top of the *Leean* road, which I used to climb over to get to the fields above *Swartifield*. Then I would skip down over the stepped braes that led to Jessie's house, a track leading part of the way down, though not on the stepped (flat) areas where the sheep grazed.

The Gibsons

In fact I had good reason to visit *Swartifield* well before my three-year spell staying there. My father had a first cousin called David Gibson – a nephew of Jessie's. He moved south and married Nettie Orr, and the couple settled in Kilmarnock. They used to come home on holiday regularly.

My great aunt Jessie always had them staying with her at *Swartifield.* I used to love playing with their daughter, Cora, who was the same age as me. We played together many's a time on the braes above *Swartifield.* I used to walk over every day with milk from *Innister* to supply the Gibsons – going in the morning so that they could use the milk to make a milk-pudding to eat at dinner-time. I did this every day when Cora was home, walking back to *Innister,* tired but happy, in the early evening.

Life at *Swartifield*

I enjoyed staying with Jessie, who was really good to me. My great-aunt always had dinner ready when I came home from school. She made particularly tasty soup, and delicious oven-scones. I would help with the washing-up, but Jessie did most of the house-work herself, being still an able woman. While at *Swartifield*, I used to go to *Swandale,* a bit further down the brae (now a ruin), to buy milk. Here lived a Grieve woman, originally from the unusually named *Fa Doun*, also situated nearby.

Before going to bed each night at nine, I would pass the evening chatting to my auntie, all the while knitting a man's sock, using wool supplied by my mother. I knitted a sock every week night, so that every Friday when I returned home to *Innister* for the weekend, I would have five socks to take home. These were duly issued, in pairs (obviously!) to my hard-working brothers.

Free Caramels

Jessie used to walk up over the braes to the main road around the same time every Saturday night, to get her messages from the Co-op van as it passed by. Jacko Linklater drove it; he lived at *Blossan* (formerly *Hammermugly*), very close to *Swartifield*, the last house in Sourin before the *Leean*. Jessie kept two sheets of lining paper at the bottom of her basket, and while at the van, without saying a word, Jacko would lift the sheets of paper and place a handful of caramels under them. A free gift for his valued customers. I always looked forward to Jessie coming back from the van, as sweeties were a rare treat, and whereas at *Innister* there were so many siblings to pass them round to, at *Swartifield* there was only me. I knew Jessie would share them with me – and she always did!

An 'o' onto Everything

Very early during my stay in Sourin, I discovered an unusual local tradition – that of putting the letter 'o' at the end of almost every forename. This custom was popular in other parts of Rousay, too, but it was most pronounced in Sourin. Thus anyone with the name Jim was called Jeemo,

Bill was Billo, and so on. The same treatment was accorded to females; Jessie became Jesso, Margaret was Maggo, Mary was Maro, etc. Yet, strangely enough, my brother Robert was never called Robbo during his time staying in Sourin; neither was Nettie referred to as Netto. I rather disliked being called Phebo, and looked forward to moving back to Wester for that reason alone![36]

Sourin Kirk

Each Friday after school, I would meet Jessie on the main road above *Swartifield*. My aunt would take my school bag, and give me the five socks I had knitted during the week, along with any other of my belongings she thought I might

---

[36] The letter 'o' was in fact set to plague me throughout my life. I have long lost count of the times that I have received letters addressing me as Phoebe (even 'correcting' my own spelling of the name). I know that Phoebe is the more popular spelling, but Phebe is not in fact uncommon.

need, and I would then walk all the way along the *Leean*, and home to *Innister* for the weekend. For that part of my time at *Swartifield* when I attended Wester school, I didn't go home every weekend, but often remained with my aunt. Jessie was a regular church-goer, as were a good number in the Sourin district in those days,[37] so it was expected that any Marwick child staying with her would go to church with her. I didn't mind going in the least. Jessie and I took a different route, though. We would walk along a rough track from *Cruannie*, above the *Ervadale* road, then down a steep grassy path to the Sourin kirk, located next to the Suso burn, and back home the same way after the service.

The Sourin kirk was originally built as a Free Church following the Disruption of 1843, its first minister being the very popular George Ritchie (after whom my grandfather was named). In those years both the Free Church and the United Presbyterian Church, located in Brinian, had congregations of impressive size, partly the result of revivalist influences on the island and elsewhere in Orkney.[38] Rousay's Free Church was eventually brought back within the Church of Scotland fold following the reunion of 1929.

---

[37] Just a generation or two previously almost every family in Sourin attended church (the vast majority adhering to the Free Kirk). It has been said that at the close of many a service, you could see the entire stretch of road from the kirk, past *Woo* and right to the crossroads at the main road, as a swathe of black, as congregants, always attired in their best dark clothes, made their way home.

[38] For more information on revivals in Orkney during this period, see Tom Lennie, '*Land of Many Revivals: Scotland's Extraordinary Legacy of Christian Revivals over Four Centuries (1527–1857)*', 2015.

The minister at the time I attended was the Rev. Robert R. Davidson, who had previously served as an army padre. He was somewhat fundamentalist in his doctrine, but he was a highly respected figure in the community. I always thought he was a really fine man. He served in Rousay for 35 years.

Some of the kirks in those days retained the tradition of having a precentor – a male singer who would stand at the front and sing out the first line of each verse, as an aid to the congregation, which would then join in. Although considered a characteristic of Gaelic culture, this tradition was nevertheless being observed in Rousay when I was a bairn. The local precentor at that time certainly had a strong voice, and he knew the hymns well. He was a tad lacking in vocal refinement however, and what has been described as his loud bellowing sometimes actually frightened young bairns present.

In her later days, Jessie moved in with Jim and Isabella at *Innister*, where she lived for a lot more years, before passing away in 1964, in her ninety-second year.

Sourin School Stories

Outsider Pupil

During my stay at *Swartifield*, when I was old enough, I attended school in Sourin. I used to walk down the long brae to school alone – though I was often accompanied by a fellow-pupil, Chrissie o'*Digro* on the way home. The Sourin school had two class-rooms compared to Wester's one. Around thirty pupils were in

attendance, which was far more than attended Wester. I initially felt quite intimidated by this, more-so because I came from outwith Sourin, and hardly knew anyone. Indeed, while I enjoyed staying at *Swartifield*, I never fully settled in at Sourin school. Despite this, I made a few good friends there who, thankfully, have remained friends into adulthood.

Sourin Teachers

At Sourin school I got a retired female teacher for a while, who was standing in until they could find a more suitable candidate. She was very old-fashioned, but I liked her. Then there was John D. Mackay from Sanday, who taught by means of postal lessons - old-fashioned distance-learning. I felt this was a poor way of working, as there was no direct communication between teacher and pupil, who never got to meet each other. And yet I must have met Mr Mackay at least once, because I remember he was a very tall, slim man.

Sharing a Custard Cream

I recall one day at school our class had done exceedingly well at some project, and as a reward, the teacher decided to give us a treat. She came forth with a big plate of custard creams. The kids were overjoyed at such rare luxury and rushed forward to grab a biscuit. Some took more than one, however. I, being somewhat retiring, and perhaps still feeling a bit of an outsider in the class, hung back until everyone else had got their booty. Then I stepped forward gingerly to the biscuit plate - only to find that all the custard creams were gone! I was so disappointed, and walked back to my seat about to burst in tears. Then Jimmy Pirie came up to me. He had taken two biscuits, but noticing I had returned to my seat empty-handed, generously offered me one of his. I was so pleased by this act of kindness, and enjoyed my custard cream all the more because of it. Jimmy's action shouldn't have surprised me – he was such a gentleman, even at that tender age – and remained so right into adult life.

Little Latin Lie

Jean, who did her turn at living with aunt Jessie a couple of years before myself, developed a particular dislike for one teacher at Sourin school – a tall burly man who had a temper to match his strong, commanding physique. When marking pupils' school work, he would often get so angry at the incorrect answers given that he would violently hurl jotters across the room towards the offending pupil. Even when writing on the blackboard, he would take aim and angrily throw his chalk at some unsuspecting victim. While never personally at the receiving end of such outburst of bad temper, Jean inwardly developed a great fear of this imposing man.

She was therefore horrified to learn that in order to further her education at Kirkwall Grammar School, our mother wanted her to take lessons in Latin in her final year at Sourin. This meant the dreaded male teacher would be instructing her. He said he couldn't fit her into his timetable, but was willing to give her a half-hour lesson at the end of the school-day, from 4 to 4.30. In truth this was a kind gesture on his behalf, but Jean dreaded being alone in a class-room with this fearsome fellow. The room itself seemed to be bigger and more daunting after all the other kids had left for home.

The lessons went well for a time and Jean was making progress. But her dread of the tutor failed to subside, and she began to plot a way of getting out of this impromptu Latin class. She plucked up the courage to tell her teacher one day that her mother had decided not to send her to Kirkwall school after all, so there was no need for her to continue learning Latin. Although surprised by this sudden outcome, the teacher had little option but stop the one-to-one tuition with immediate effect. Jean felt instant relief that she could now leave the classroom at the same time as her fellow-pupils. Her mother, of course, was none too pleased at her dropping out, though she was almost definitely never told the true reason for it!

Courier Service

I remember once during my time at Sourin school, the teacher giving me a letter and asking me to drop it off at the Wester school-house on my way back to *Innister* for the weekend. Naturally, I did as I was bade. Two

115

days later, on the Sunday, as I started out on the long journey back to *Swartifield*, who should I see coming out of *Cogar* to meet me than the Wester teacher, Miss Sutherland. She had obviously gone across from the school-house to watch through *Cogar*'s window for me coming along the road from *Innister*. She would have had no idea when I might pass by, for my times of departure varied considerably – sometimes it was in the afternoon, sometimes early evening. But there she was, and she handed me a box, asking me to take it to Ms Mowat at the Sourin school. Of course, I didn't dare open it, but I was very curious to know what was inside. It turned out to be nothing more exciting than a box of pen-nibs, the Sourin school having run out of them. My courier services were highly appreciated. I decided, however, not to share the story with my class-mates for fear they considered me a teacher's pet!

Accidents and Illnesses

Bread-Knife

I mind all the family sitting around the table eating one

day, when Roderick, just a boy, started fooling around with the bread-knife. He pretended he had cut his hand, and invited me to pull the knife away. I did so, but somehow in the process Roderick's finger did actually get cut! I was no doubt partly to blame, though so, unquestionably, was Roderick for playing around with a sharp instrument with so young a child. Either way, he never blamed me for the accident – but it certainly taught him a lesson, and I never remember him fooling around with the bread-knife again!

Marks on my Body!

I have collected various marks on my hands and feet, each the result of an accident occasioned during my childhood. The first occurred when I was just five. It was breakfast-time, and mum had made a pot of porridge, from which she dished a plate for me. Then, busy as she ever was, she went out to milk the kye in the byre. When I finished my serving, I went to spoon some more into my bowl from the large pot simmering on the stove. In the process, some boiling porridge dropped from the spoon onto my bare foot, instantly blistering my soft skin. I shrieked in pain, and one of my sisters ran for mum. I had burnt my foot badly, and required the nurse to come and apply a bandage dressing. In fact, so affected was I by this accident that I was off school for over a month. 85 years later, the scar can still be seen on my left foot.

On another occasion Nettie and I were arguing over who could have a particular pencil (which I think, with hindsight, actually belonged to my sister). I had a firm grip of it, though Nettie was pulling at it for all her worth. tugging the pencil back and forth for a time like that, a piece of lead got lodged in my hand, before Nettie finally pulled it free and ran off with it. That piece of lead remains lodged under the skin of my hand to this very day. It has never come out.

On a third occasion some years later, I was trying to open a can of stove-polish in order to polish the stove in *Innister*'s kitchen. The top wouldn't budge. Using all my might to loosen it, it eventually gave way all of a sudden – cutting my finger in the process. A small black scar has remained visible on the tip of one of my fingers ever since.

Shot at!

One summer's day, most of the Marwicks were out in the field across from the *Saviskaill* field known as *Kuiv*,[39] singling neeps. Suddenly, a sound whistled menacingly through the air, and with it, the sound of gunfire, breaking the stillness of the fine July morning, Someone had actually fired a gun towards us, literally missing my sister, Betty and I by just a foot or two at most. What a fright we all got; for some seconds I stood in a state of shock. Quickly coming to terms with what had just happened, Roderick stalked across the fields in the direction of the gunshot, ready to have it out with whoever was responsible for this reckless act. He found a neighbour outside his home with a rifle; just as horrified at what had occurred as we were. It had been a terrible accident; he hadn't meant to fire his gun - and he was utterly apologetic. Back in the field, we had little option but carry on with our work, now much more aware than before of the potential hazards of singling neeps!

---

[39] The field of *Kuiv*, along with the three other fields that converge at the bottom of *Innister's* road, are regarded as containing the richest and deepest soil to be found anywhere on Rousay, being of a pure black hue associated with soil purity.

The Measles

Roderick worked really hard at *Innister*, not least when the whole Marwick clan took ill with the measles. He was just fourteen at the time. Roderick was the first to catch the disease and was laid up in bed for a while. But soon after, all the family, including my mother, was struck with the illness, each member being confined to bed. It was during this period, aged just nine, that, stuck in my room and with nothing else to do, I knitted my first jersey, a fair achievement for a girl so tender in years.

Poor Bill suffered from terrible hallucinations during his spell with the measles. (He would cry out for help, insisting his head was tied to a fencing post). No-one was more relieved than he when his condition eventually began to slowly improve. By this time Roderick's condition was also improving, and he forced himself to get up and go and attend to all the work on the farm, which just had to get done, for everyone else in the family was still laid up in bed.

Roderick did an awful lot himself at this time, but was helped in the hay-work and haystack building by men from nearby farmsteads, who always looked out for one another; keen to lend a hand when others were in need. However, none of them stayed at *Innister* for tea or anything on this occasion – they were keen to get away as quickly as possible for fear of infection; measles being a particularly dreaded illness in these days, with no known cure or preventative medication. It was seen as much worse than, e.g. the mumps.

The Mumps

My brother Robert referred to another occasion when he contracted the mumps a few days before returning home to Rousay from Kirkwall school for the long summer holidays. This caused consternation on the island. No one could remember when there had last been a case of mumps on Rousay, so there was little or no immunity to it from residents on the island. A few other Marwicks caught the disease from Robert, with the consequence that *Innister*'s folk were almost completely ostracised by the rest of the community for most of the summer (which was actually well past the period of any risk of further infection taking place). During this period, however, our older brother, Sydney was home on holiday from Wick. Having had the mumps many years previously, he didn't take too kindly to being refused entry to a dance in Sourin that he had so looked forward to attending. Although he protested that there was no fear of infection, he was barred from entering the hall. Deeply disappointed, he was forced to return home to *Innister* on his own.

Knock and Tumble

Aged around fourteen, my sister, Anna worked for a while at *Feolquoy* (between *Cogar* and *Langskaill*) to an elderly woman named Jenny. Anna's bedroom was upstairs, and, aged just eight, I went to visit her one day; whereupon Anna took me upstairs to her room. Of course, there was no electric lighting in those days, and even oil lamps were few in number (because of the cost of fuel). So it was getting gye dark when I left Anna's room to head for home. At the top of the stairs I leant forward to open the door I was sure was there. But there was no door, and I went tumbling down the stairs, landing in a heap at the bottom with an unceremonious thud. Though rather shaken, I was nevertheless none the worse for wear. I quickly picked myself up, and proceeded on my way back to *Innister*, deciding not to share anything of my undignified 'short trip' with the rest of the family!

Klaes

Clothes-Making

As well as sewing, my mother did a lot of knitting. She knitted jerseys for all the family, long stockings for the girls, and thick socks for her sons. She used a circular knitting machine, fairly popular in those days. But even with this aid, knitting a jersey was no easy task. Mother would knit three panels for the front of the jersey and three for the back. Then she had to sew them all together, as she did the arms, the cuffs, the waistband and the neckband. She always made a perfect job of this. Virtually all of her offspring got a new jersey each year after the summer holidays, to wear for the new term at school. (Each child would also get a new pair of fine leather boots at least every other year. This seems quite extravagant, but it would be the only decent footwear we had to our name, worn day-in, day-out, until they were well past their best).

New Coat

I well remember, when aged around fourteen, Jean being given a new coat – which our mother bought for her in Kirkwall. In turn I, a couple of years younger, was offered Jean's old coat – which had originally been sewn together by our mother. Devastated that my sister was getting a brand new coat and I a home-spun reject, I went into a corner and gret for ages.

On a later, happier occasion, my mother went to Kirkwall, having promised to buy a dress for me. I was so excited about getting a new dress that I set myself to work for it. I spent the whole day that my mother was away working in the house – from seven in the morning till her return around six-thirty at night. I was utterly exhausted when she arrived back. But it all proved well worthwhile – she returned home with a beautiful dress, complete with brooch; a source of pride and joy to a thankful young girl for many a day.

Neeptians & All-Blacks

Few folk have even heard of the apparel nowadays, but I mind my aunt Jessie always wore a neeptian - a large black head-square with a fringe, that went round her head and was then tied at the back of her neck so that it remained in place. Neeptians were common to women of my great-aunt's generation, but were already going out of fashion in

122

my childhood, because I don't ever remember my mother wearing one, for example. They pre-existed the head-square, which only came into fashion at a later date, and which my peers and I used to wear. Head-squares were smaller than neeptians, were tied differently, were more varied in colour, and had no fringe.

But although my mother never wore black neeptians, she did, following the death of my father, insist on dressing completely in black. This accorded to a custom of the day after a death in the family, and my mother adhered to it most particularly, whether in public or at home. This was in stark contrast to her younger years, when she loved to wear light-coloured clothes. But for the sixteen years between her husband's death and her own, day-in, day-out, my mother's coat, dresses, blouses, hat, stockings and shoes were all black (as can be seen from the last known photograph taken of her, in 1948 – see photo section).

Secky Brats & Footos

A further form of clothing that you never hear tell of, nor see sight of, nowadays is a secky brat. This was simply a crude form of peenie (apron) – a hessian sack cut up, with bands sewn on at either side, and tied around the waist. Women wore them (sometimes on top of overalls) to keep their clothes clean when doing their housework or farm work. My mother wore a secky brat almost every day, as did virtually all the women of Rousay in those days. Hardly a dainty or fashionable garment, it was nevertheless very practical.

Yet another article of clothing common when I was peedie, but little heard of nowadays – was to be found at the other end of the human anatomy from neeptians – footos. Footos were simply thick ankle socks that Rousay farmfolk wore over another pair of socks, for added warmth and comfort when working out on the farm all day in their rubber boots.

Buyin' Klaes

With no clothes shop on Rousay, and trips to Kirkwall relatively rare, my mother ordered a lot of her family's clothes out of catalogues that were sent from firms like *J. D. Williams* and *Oxendales*, both of Manchester.

Additionally, some of the draper businesses from mainland Orkney, such as *D. H. Gorn's* of Kirkwall and *P. L. Johnston's* of Stromness, came to Rousay from time to time with suitcases full of various clothes samples, for women, men and children. This suited the great majority of islanders, who rarely got the opportunity to make the trip to Kirkwall. After orders were made it usually took two or three weeks for the goods to arrive on the island. Wester orders were despatched in one large delivery to the shop at *Quoyostray*. News of its arrival quickly spread through the parish, and in no time scores of folk gathered at the shop, eager to obtain their purchases. It was a big event in Wester (as it would have been in other

Rousay districts, too), and there was certainly plenty of excitement within the Marwick household on such occasion.

Hand-me Downs

Every two years or so David and Nettie Gibson sent home to Rousay an enormous hamper of used but very good clothes for the men and women of *Innister*. What a boon this was to my family – saving us a lot of money. The hamper was sent to *Swartifield*, so aunt Jessie got the pick of the post. But she didn't have much time to look through the clothes, for us young Marwicks would come swarming over to snatch our share as soon as we heard the hamper had arrived! It was certainly a big occasion for my siblings and I, and we would proudly return home with our spoils, which would last us for most of the coming year.

As well as these hand-me-downs, one year the Gibsons also sent Jean and I, as Christmas presents, two brand new hoods, known as pixies. In fact we were perhaps the first on the island to wear this fashionable head-gear, which soon became popular all over Rousay (and indeed throughout Orkney), almost everyone owning one.

Stories Galore

Jammy Piece

After leaving school, Roderick worked for a time at a nearby croft, and as such, he was provided with his meal at the top of the day. One lunchtime, seated round the table, he spread some butter on his slice of bread, then spread jam on top of that, as was his custom, and he munched heartily into it. The elderly lady of the house instantly reprimanded him for spreading butter and jam on a single piece of bread, which she saw as a foul, uncivilised habit.

The next day, around the same table, Maggie-Ann watched closely, as Roderick again spread butter on his piece of bread. But then he took another slice and spread jam on that. He closed the two pieces together, and ate to his heart's content. Maggie-Ann was horrified, but couldn't tell him off, for he hadn't violated her order not to spread butter and jam on the same piece of bread!

Bike-Ride to Sourin

After saving his wages for a long period, Roderick was able to buy a motor-bike. One Friday evening when we were both intending to go to Sourin for a dance, I remember him offering me a lift on the back of it. I gladly accepted the offer, saving me from having to walk all that distance. Being young and laddish, Roderick didn't exactly travel slowly, and I quickly felt uneasy, precariously balanced as I was on the back of his bike, something I had never done before in

my life. When riding round a tight corner at perhaps greater speed than was wise, Roderick naturally leaned the bike over to one side. Thinking it was going to topple over, I spontaneously leaned in the other direction. This unsettled Roderick, who up to that point felt he was in full control of his vehicle. When we arrived at the Sourin hall he let it be known in no uncertain terms that I wasn't exactly the easiest passenger to be carrying on his bike! He never offered me a lift again - and I never dared to ask for one!

Buying 'The Orcadian'

Every Thursday after school, my mother got me to pop in along a particular house in Wester to get *The Orcadian* so that all the Marwick family could catch up on all the news from other parts of Orkney. In the house lived an elderly woman who was known to have a bit of a temper. She had an unusual nick-name, the meaning of which I never knew, and which I've never since heard in any context, and yet which somehow felt quite appropriate! One week I wasn't sent to get the paper. The following Thursday, when I turned up at the door, the woman of the house gave me a right telling-off. *'I can't afford to keep buyin' the pipper if you're no'*

ga'an to come and pay for it!' Blah blah, blah. Although she had a fair point, I was just a wee girl, and was both hurt and intimidated by this verbal offload. It wasn't my fault – if there was a problem she should have got on to my mother about it, not me. I always found it hard to like the woman after that.

Galloping *Prince*

My sister, Anna loved horses, and was very good with them (a passion inherited by some of her own offspring). She adored *Prince*, the family horse. She was sitting on *Prince*'s back one day but couldn't get the animal to move forward. Encourage or goad it as she might, it simply wouldn't budge. Donald was watching on. He had a cunning plan. Into the house he went, and came back out a moment or two later with a darning needle in hand. Before Anna could protest, he stuck the needle into *Prince*'s rear end. The horse bolted, taking a helpless Anna with it, galloping down the farm road. It finally came to a stop without poor Anna falling off. She was, however, somewhat shaken, her face as white as a sheet. As you might imagine, she had a few words to say to her peedie brother when she got back on terra firma! Indeed, if only she had hold of that same darning needle, there's little doubt to whose rear end she might have securely attached it - and it certainly wouldn't have been any four-legged friend! Thankfully,

though, the incident failed to dampen Anna's love of *Prince* or of horses generally.

What a Racket!

I well remember, when in my mid-teens, my cousin, Margaret, coming over from the mainland with her three bairns to stay at *Innister* for a break while her husband was serving in the Forces. Where everyone slept I can't quite remember. But it was great fun to have them.

During one visit, wee John was making a racket, blowing the whistle he had recently been given. I was in the kitchen baking bere-bannocks, when John came bounding in. As I was bending to lift the iron yetlin from the stove, John blasted his noisy whistle right in my ear. What a piercing sound. I could have seen the peedie blighter far enough! As it was, I snatched the offending instrument from his hand and set it up on the mantelpiece – well out of his reach. Annoyed at the theft of his toy, John stood tall, hands on his sides, staring up at my face. *'Gae me my whistle'*, he demanded, *'or I'll stick yer bannocks doon yer throat'*! I was slightly taken aback that a boy so young would speak to someone three times his age with such authority. But the whole household enjoyed a good laugh, and John did get his whistle back – eventually!

Making a Phone-call

Next to nobody had a phone in their homes in those days. It was possible to make phone-calls – at a charge – from the

local Post Office. By the time I had reached my mid-teens, there was one other household in Wester that had recently installed a phone, and they were happy for folk in the community to use it for a significantly lesser charge. Some Wester folk felt, however, that the main reason for such generosity was that, fine folk as they were, they were rather keen to catch up on the local gossip! It was common knowledge, for example, that the woman of the house would often stand in the hallway while someone was making a call, only a thin partition separating her from the caller.

On one occasion, I was visiting this home with one or two others from *Innister*. We were all seated around the fire. At some point I asked if I could phone my brother, Bill, who then worked at *Swanbister* in Orphir, and who liked to keep in touch with his family back home. At the time some of my clothing vouchers, issued during the war years, had mysteriously gone missing from my bedroom. Still feeling raw at the loss of my coupons, I shared the story with Bill. Having finished the call, and sitting back around the fireplace, after a while old Kathy suddenly asked, *'How's everyone's clothing coupons lasting?'* I didn't say a word, sensing instantly the motive for this unusual question – Kathy had once again been listening in on a private conversation!

Let it Snow

We got far more snow in Rousay when I was peedie than we do now, and it seemed to stay far longer. Not infrequently, the *Leean* road would get completely blocked, up to three or four feet deep, and for many days on end. Of course there was no snow-plough on the island then, and it would have been impossible to have driven a horse and cart through the deep snow. On such occasions, one or two of the Marwick men, along with a couple of men from neighbouring farms, used to meet together after an early dinner, and trudge their way through the snow right up over the *Leean* and down to the Co-op shop, which was located next to the Sourin school. Here they would buy such necessities as their homes had run out of – paraffin-oil, bread, etc, and carry it in bags back home across the hill – a lengthy and laborious round trip.

Ghost in White

The cows needed milking by hand every morning and night. One dark evening Betty and I went out around nine o'clock to perform this duty. Betty did the milking while I held a lantern above her so that she could see. I was just a young girl at the time – Betty was a good few years older. When we had finished, we left the byre; Betty carrying a full bucket of fresh milk, myself holding the lantern in front of her. As we exited the byre, suddenly a large white object appeared at the side of us; swaying quickly back and fore.

131

Instantly terrified, and under the impression we were genuinely encountering a ghost, Betty and I screamed and

made a dash back to the house, milk splashing everywhere. When we got to the house, our buckets nearly empty, we heard uproarious laughter behind us. It was one of my relatives - who had arrived on the scene, fully draped in a white sheet, and who had been waiting outside the byre for us to appear, seeking a laugh at our expense. They certainly got that.

On another occasion, all of my family went out after dinner to work in the harvest, as was customary at that time of year. Feeling unwell, the same relative remained in the house, and sat on a chair on the landing at the top of the stairs, reading a book. Eventually, after a few hours of work, I came back in to get the lantern from upstairs. It was late in the evening, and so it was gye dark. I climbed to the top of the stairs, and reached to grab the lantern. As I did so, suddenly a large white form shifted to my side. It scared the living daylights out of me, for I thought there was nobody in the house but myself. I almost fell back over and have often wondered that I could easily have gone tumbling down several flights of stairs as a result of my relative's prank. The two of us never fell out over this issue, however, though I have retained a fear of the dark ever since.

Day Trips

I had never set foot off of the island of my birth until the age of fourteen or fifteen, when I made my first trip to Kirkwall. Even then it was just for the day. The boat left Rousay pier (then situated in Frotoft) at twenty-past-eight, and returned from Evie around six. On my first ever trip to 'the big city', I went with my sisters, Anna and Jean, and we had to walk all the way to the Rousay pier - over an hour's walk from *Innister*. I as yet had no job and so owned no money.[40] Jean offered me a half-crown – a substantial sum for a fourteen-year-old to receive in those days. In truth she could ill-afford to give it, for although working at that time, she didn't earn much. I never forgot this act of kindness. What fun we young girls had in Kirkwall, not least me on my inaugural visit. We even decided to mark the occasion by getting our photo taken – at Jim Sinclair's studio at the top of the Strynd (see photo section). On another memorable

---

[40] I never had any money while I lived at home. Indeed, right up to leaving Rousay at age of twenty, I never had a penny to my name. I didn't get paid for work at *Innister* – but got my 'keep' (board & lodgings), which I considered good enough. Nor do I remember any of my brothers getting paid during the years they stayed and worked at home.

occasion I went to Kirkwall for the day with my school-friend, Evelyn.

Tom o'*Banks* operated a ferry service to and from the mainland. His boat sailed from a wee slipway at Frotoft and docked at the Evie pier, further north than the current ferry terminal at Tingwall. There weren't many days Tom's boat didn't sail – he ventured out in all weathers. This suited most islanders, but made for a sometimes rather adventurous crossing! In addition, several times when I was a teenager crossing back to Rousay, Tom couldn't get the boat near enough to the shore, so passengers had to wade ashore on foot – getting our feet and legs soaked in the process. We never thought anything of the inconvenience – in any case there was no other option.

I rarely had the opportunity of visiting Rousay's neighbouring islands. But I did make it to Egilsay once in my teenage years; this to visit my friend, Violet (who I first met at a dance in Rousay). She invited me over to the Egilsay picnic. I mind getting a lift to Sourin from Nurse Park, and waiting in *Hurtiso* for the boat to leave (even though I hardly knew the folk that lived there!). It was just a tiny boat that crossed from Sourin to Egilsay. Arriving on the island, Violet met me at the pier, and we walked straight to the picnic. There was a dance to follow, and I thoroughly enjoyed the whole experience. I have to confess, though, that apart from paying a brief stop at the pier, I have never been to Wyre to this day.

Westside Jaunts

Brigsend

I used to walk many's the time to visit Johnny and Rita at *Brigsend,* on Rousay's Westside, where Johhny worked after leaving *Innister.* I would walk back home at night when it would be getting gye dark. It was a long and lonely walk – the totally uninhabited area around Quandal being a particularly eerie place at night. At one point I stayed for around three weeks at *Brigsend* when Rita was nearing the end of her second pregnancy, helping out around the house with all sorts of chores.

One day I was in the scullery washing the dishes, when I suddenly heard the sound of bleating. I looked out the window, certain a sheep had broken into the garden. But there was nothing there. It took me a wee while to realise that the bleating was coming not from outside, but from *inside* the house. Rita had just given birth to a beautiful baby daughter, Margaret (my first niece), and it was her fledgling, tender cries I was hearing! I've joked with Margaret many's the time since then about having mistaken her for a sheep!

Although I wasn't expecting to get paid for my help, I was given £4 & 10 shillings when I left *Brigsend.* I thought this an extremely generous gift, for I knew Johnny could ill afford it. Hugely appreciative of my earnings, I bought a new coat with the money.[41]

---

[41] I also used to visit Jim Yorston (my 1st cousin) and his wife at *Quoygrinnie*, also on the Westside, (formerly inhabited by the Houries).

Rattling Johnny

I remember few stories specifically relating to my brother, Johnny. But I do recall one night, when he and Rita cycled from *Brigsend* to *Innister* one evening. Johnny had a few drinks in him (which in itself was unusual – and he very rarely got drunk). He was clearly rather tipsy, and as he and Rita cycled home I remember him swaying about a bit on the road and singing out, *'I'm rattling, I'm rattling, I'm rattling on the seat of my bike'*! I found it a great fun to see my older brother carefree and enjoying himself so much.

Sometimes when I was staying at Johnny's, I would cycle with Maissie o'*Westness* to a dance over in the Sourin Hall – half-way round the island (the hall was situated right across the road from the school, along with several houses, most of which are now gone, though the hall is still standing). We would pick up Edith Gibson from the shop at *Hullion* on the way.[42] I didn't own my own bike, but would borrow Rita's. What fun we had. We would cycle back home in the early hours of the following morning

---

[42] At the time of writing, Edith is 92, and still living in the *Hullion* district.

(though probably not in as straight a line as our outward journey!).

Renie's Party

Renie was a close friend of Evelyn and they were both the same age. Renie's family had moved from *Maybank* (which has since become one of Rousay's 'vanished' houses), and now lived at *Quoygrinnie*, an isolated house in the Westside district, along the road from *Westness*. Here her father served as game-keeper to *Trumland Estate* (the former stately residence of the notorious General F.W. Traill-Burroughs). Renie held a party on her eighteenth birthday, to which all her female friends were invited, including one or two who came all the way from Kirkwall. Evelyn's dad owned a motor-bike with a side car, and after the party had finished, he offered to take both me and Evelyn home together. Though a bit wary of motor-bike rides following my earlier experience with Roderick, I accepted his offer of a lift, as it would save me a long, lonely walk home. One of us sat on the pillion-seat, clinging onto Peemo; while the other had the comparative luxury of riding in the side-car. I managed to survive the journey!

Peemo let me off at *Tou*, from where I walked onwards to *Innister*. Because it was dark, I decided to walk along the road, rather than take a short-cut through the fields via *Breckan*. Suddenly I saw the movements of a torch-light from a field ahead of me, quite some distance from any dwelling-place. Wondering who on earth could be wondering about in the fields at this time on a cold dark night, I became absolutely terrified and started running towards *Innister*. It turned out to be a neighbour, out checking his snares for rabbits. But I wasn't to know that at the time, and I can tell you, I was never so glad to arrive home in my life!

The War

I was twelve when the Second World War broke out. The conflict seemed to go on forever, continuing through most of my teenage years. Because farming was regarded as an essential service, most young men engaged in that occupation - at least on larger farms – were exempt from National Service. Thus, most of my brothers, who worked either at *Innister* or on other farms, were not called into the Forces. There were three exceptions in the Marwick household - Sydney, David and Robert. None of these were engaged in reserved occupations when the war broke out, and so all three were conscripted into service.

David was called into the Royal Air Force, where he served as an instructor of bomber wireless operators based in *Dreghorn Barracks*, Edinburgh.[43] Sydney served in the

---

[43] My first cousins, Hugh & John Yorston (sons of my aunt Bella) both also served in the Royal Air Force, as pilots. Hugh's achievement during the war period was remarkable – totalling a noteworthy 400 flying hours in Tiger-Moths, Harvards, Hurricanes and, his favourite, Spitfires (in sorties variably performed in South Africa, India and Burma). Johnnie

Royal Artillery as a sergeant instructor for most of the war, also on mainland Scotland. Meanwhile, Robert was the youngest Marwick son to be called into the Forces, joining the army at the age of eighteen and spending most of the war years half a world away. Accorded the impersonal 'name' 2389442, or 442 for short, he served as a radio-engineer in the Royal Corps of Signals for four-and-a-half years, three of which were spent in India.

Rationing

The war years were extremely difficult times in many ways, but the hardships we faced in Rousay were miniscule compared to what so many folk suffered elsewhere. Everyone was affected during these years by strict rationing of food and other household items. The amount of sugar we could buy was restricted to 8oz per adult per week (for all purposes). As a conscientious young girl living at *Swartifield* at the time, I felt guilty about taking sugar in my tea. So I decided one day I should do without it, and I've never taken any sugar in my tea since that day. Flour was also rationed, and for most of the war years we never saw white flour. Instead we were offered flour of a lower quality, grey-brown in colour.

---

served as a rear gunner in both Lancasters and Wellingtons and was later awarded the Africa Star and Clasp. (See also *'Hugh Yorston: Diaries of a Fighter Pilot'*, edited by Brian Halcro & privately distributed).

Sweets were also rationed, though my mother always ensured that Nettie got her meagre weekly portion, bless her.

Everyone received a clothes-ration book, containing 24 coupons, which was to last for at least six or seven months. An overcoat used up around 18 coupons, a jacket 13, a nightie 6, a petticoat 3, stockings 3 and a pair of pants 3. It was the same for civilian women everywhere in the country. I kept hold of my clothes-ration book as a memento for many a day after the war finally ended.

Mock Raid

My mother felt an especial attachment to the war effort owing to the fact that three of her sons served in the Forces during World War II. So concerned was my mother in regards to her sons' welfare and to the war effort in general that she would sit by the radio every evening at six and listen intently to the latest war news as it was broadcast across the airwaves.

Then one day my mother's connection with the war was brought much nearer to home. The British Army decided to engage in a mock raid on Rousay. A unit of twenty-one soldiers was posted on the island. As part of their mission they came over to Wasbister, and the men trooped up *Innister*'s road, quite a sight to behold on the hinder-side of a quiet Orkney island. The soldiers stopped on the green in front of the auld farm house, and my mother went out to speak with them.

With three sons serving in the war, [44] so proud was she of the Forces that despite being slightly overwhelmed at the thought of feeding so many men, she was quick to offer them refreshments. They eagerly accepted her offer. Oatcakes, pancakes, scones, bere-bannocks (a delightful novelty to them) – all home-baked of course - were all offered to the squad of hungry soldiers. And boy were they hungry. They scoffed everything, clearing my mother of every item of baking in the house. But she didn't grudge it for a moment – being keen to help out in any way she could.

---

[44] There was very nearly a fourth Marwick recruit to the war effort. Born in 1924, Donald was only 15 when the war broke out. Working as a farm servant in South Ronaldsay at the time, he nobly decided he wanted to join the Forces, just as three of his older brothers had done. He even crossed over to Caithness in an attempt to sign up. Marching orders came, however, not from an army officer on mainland Scotland, but from his own mother back home! Hearing of his laudable intentions, but knowing he was too young to sign up, she ordered him back home with immediate effect!

Rousay Casualties

All homes had to buy special black-out curtains, to stop houses being spotted by enemy aircraft. My mother was very particular about ensuring that no lamp was lit unless we were sure the windows were thoroughly covered, and that no light could escape.

I remember the distinctive drone of German airplanes flying over Rousay at night-time during the war – a sound I never forgot. They would wake me up when I was in bed at night, and I was scared to go back to sleep. My friend, Evelyn remembered seeing them high in the sky even during daytime at school – usually three at a time; their engines making a pronounced thud that was easily recognisable, and quite scary.

The dangers of war were particularly brought home to Wester school bairns when the first bombing raid took place over Orkney, which led to the first civilian casualty of the war on British soil. This victim turned out to be our teacher's brother in law, and the tragedy made Rousay pupils very aware of the sober realities of combat.

Plane Crash

One Sunday morning during the war a British plane with two men on board was flying south over the north isles when it ran into difficulty. Approaching the north coast of Rousay, the pilot was forced to attempt a crash landing. He thought he wasn't going to reach dry ground before his aircraft failed completely. Remarkably, he had as little as six foot to spare when the wheels of his plane touched the ground by the cliffs at the back of *Sketquoy* in Wester. Although the ground was extremely uneven, the pilot somehow managed to bring the plane to a stop without serious injury to either men.

The crash-landing created a most unearthly sound, however, which resonated for a good distance around. I mind it as weel as can be. Roderick and Jim immediately stopped their work and ran across the *Brings* towards the plane. As they approached they saw the pilot and co-pilot standing on top of the dyke and shouting, *'We're alright! We're alright!'* Although no one was hurt, the incident created a great stir in the Wester community for quite a while.

Being wartime, fuel was being strictly rationed. This was unwelcome restriction for the increasing number of young motor-bike owners on the island, who were unable to obtain petrol for their bikes. It wasn't long before word got round that someone had made their way to the scene of the impromptu landing in the night-time and syphoned off the remaining fuel from the plane for their own use. Such illegal action immediately prompted the authorities to post an armed guard to the scene to hinder further interference until such time as the plane could be removed.

On another war-time occasion a Hurricane airplane ran into difficulties while flying northwards over Sourin. It crashed into the hillside near *The Blossom*, whereupon the engine broke off and tumbled menacingly headlong down the braes, finally stopping on level ground by *Swartifield*. My aunt Jessie got an awful fright, poor dear. Locals rushed to the scene of the crash, and finding the pilot unconscious, carried him to *Digro* on a makeshift stretcher - an old wooden door. He was kept under medical assistance at *Digro* for three weeks, before being transferred to Kirkwall Balfour Hospital. Here he made a good recovery other than suffering from marked memory loss.

They say accidents occur in threes. Remarkably for such a small island, yet another significant accident involving a Royal Air Force plane in Rousay occurred towards the end of the war, again in Sourin. Tragically, this one had more serious consequences, killing both men on board.[45]

War Hut

I weel mind several Wester men being employed during the war to keep watch over the *Bay o'Saviskaill*, an easy entry point onto the island for anyone with ill intent and a boat.[46] A small wooden hut (around twelve foot square) was specially erected at the top of the cliffs at the *Head o'Saviskaill*, and local men like Sandy Donaldson o'*Vacquoy*, his next-door-neighbour, Sandy Pearson, and Peemo

---

[45] See www.rousayremembered/sourin-part-3 for more details.

[46] A similar hut was positioned at the Head o'*Farraclett*. After the war it was relocated to the farm of *Bigland*, where it usefully served as a large garden shed right up to the 1980s.

Feolquoy used to take turns, on a rota basis, at keeping watch from this lonely location. I used to see Sandy Donaldson making his way to the observation post around six o'clock each evening (he cycled part-way, then had to walk the rest). After a long shift, someone else would take over. The hut soon became a gathering point for the men-folk of the parish. I mind my brother, Jim, along with Freddie o'*Quoyostray* and others, congregating there, and whiling away the long dark nights with a blether and a laugh - and a cup of tea to wash it all down.

Serving in France

Families of those serving in the war always looked forward to receiving letters from their loved ones on active duty in various parts of the world. Jock Gibson from *Hullion* was one who had been called into the army. After a long stint in Africa, he was now serving in northern France. Whenever a letter from him arrived on Rousay, word spread quickly, for everyone was keen to hear news of his well-being. In one letter Jock wrote of his delight at bumping into Roy Russell, another Rousay lad serving in France. It was a great comfort to both to meet up, given that both were naturally feeling rather homesick so far away from Orkney. Jock wrote of how he and Roy managed to obtain flour one day, and their decision to attempt to bake pancakes in the army field kitchen, just as they had seen their mothers do in Rousay when they were bairns. They did their best with the ingredients available, but the

shortage of sugar meant they had to bake without this essential ingredient. '*Sugar or no sugar*', Jock wrote in his letter back home, '*believe you me, those pancakes were right damn good!*'

They were the last pancakes Jock was ever to eat, let alone bake. I'll never forget the day towards the end of the war when Roderick came into *Innister* with the news that Jock o'*Hullion* had been killed in action in Le Havre. He was just twenty-five. It was a terribly sad day for Rousay, and although I didn't know Jock, I knew his family, and the incident etched deeply in my youthful mind.

Welcome Home Dinner

Thankfully, all but two of the twenty or so Rousay men and women (for there were one or two females, too) who served in the Forces *did* come back home after their years of service, able now to make a welcome return to civilian life. Rousay was proud of its wartime heroes, and to show its gratitude, a reception was given for them in the Sourin hall. Robert, freshly home from his three years' stint in India, was still a single man, and he chose me as his partner. It was a grand affair – a full sit-down meal for service-men and their partners; some speeches, and then a dance, which was open to all on the island. And a great many came – indeed it proved to be one of the biggest do's in Rousay in many years.

This showed the community's gratitude to the significant contribution made by service personnel from just one small island to a war that broke out so far away from its own quiet shores. The only taint to the evening's merriment was the absence of men like Jock Gibson and Tommy Walls[47] – young men who had bravely given their lives that the rest of us might enjoy peace and freedom. We dutifully honoured them by observing a minute's silence and offering a prayer.

Peedie Black Things

On a much lighter note, I well recall an occasion towards the end of the war, when a neighbour, Agnes, was visiting my mother at *Innister*. While many food products during the war years had only been available in strictly rationed amounts, many others hadn't been available at all. Now some of these food items were on offer again. It was a Tuesday and the grocer-van had just been around the houses of Wester. My mother commented that she had bought some currants from the van, which hadn't been available for some time. She asked Agnes if she, too, had bought some. *'Currants?'* asked Agnes, innocently. *'My gosh, was that them peedie black things?"* Because of the rationing, she had apparently forgotten what currants were. Many's the time while doing a baking in later years, I would refer to currants as *'them peedie black things'*.

---

[47] Tommy was a son of the former Rousay *Co-op* manager. He was taken prisoner at the fall of Singapore in February 1942, and under Japanese rule was forced to work on the Burma-Siam railway under conditions of sheer slavery. He died just a month before Japan's surrender.

Post-War Boom

After the end of the Second World War, considerable
optimism pervaded the nation; following six gruelling years
of fighting, depression and austerity, things were now
looking up. The economy was buoyant, and this confidence
thankfully spread as far north as Rousay. Indeed, my
mother regarded the year 1946-47 as the best she ever had
in farming. Although she was stepping back to allow her
son Jim to manage *Innister*, she nonetheless felt confident
that if she could run the farm for a few years more, she
would have done very well with the prevailing prices. For
example, poultry, with which my mother worked extremely
hard over many years, was currently good business. In the
immediate post-war years farms were selling hens' eggs to
the *Kirkwall Packing Station* for four shillings & sixpence a
dozen – or just over £6 for a thirty dozen box.

Other livestock were also fetching good prices. Three of
Innister's fat heifers and one fat cow sold for a total of £194
in the autumn of '47; the heifers being graded super-special.
Mother sold wool around the same time for 5/6 per fleece
for the bigger part, and 4 shillings for the rest. Lambs

148

realised £4 per head. These were the highest prices gained in many years, and a welcome boon after successive years of economic depression. Nevertheless, we were all fully aware that, given the costs and amount of work involved, profits weren't nearly as high as an onlooker might assume. Post-war boom or not, it was still hard work eking out a living from farm work in one of Orkney's north isles.

Leaving Rousay

When my brother Jim, soon to take over the running of *Innister*, announced that he was to marry his fiancé, Isabella Lyon towards the close of 1947, I felt I would no longer be needed at home. Billo Gibson was keen that I come to *Hullion*, to work as housemaid, so that his wife could work in the shop and Post Office. Admittedly, I was attracted by the offer, for although I was only being offered £2 a week, this included board and lodgings. Thus, it was £2 more than I was currently receiving (and for what would probably be significantly lighter work). However, Billo had evidently applied to the Labour Exchange also, for they sent word that another young Rousay woman would be coming to work with him for a month's trial.

I pondered my options carefully. It didn't take too long to make the big decision. I was going to spread my wings and move away from the island of my birth. I left Rousay towards the close of 1947, aged twenty, to settle and work on the Orkney mainland. Initially, I went even further afield, for I was asked to go and stay with my brother, David in Wester Ross, for three months, to help out when his wife, Marjory was pregnant with their second child. David had become headmaster of an agricultural college in the village of Balmacara, near Kyle of Lochalsh. I really enjoyed my time there – the longest time in my life, in fact, that I have ever stayed outside Orkney. I celebrated my 21st birthday in Balmacara, my brother treating Marjory and myself to a delightful boat trip up the beautiful Loch Alsh on my special day. It was in fact a special day for Marjory, too, being her 30th birthday. A baby boy, Michael, was born to my hosts just two days later, on Monday the 29th March 1948.

When Jim and Isabella took over the running of *Innister*, my mother reserved the three upstairs rooms for her own use. As she fast approached her 65th birthday, she confided in a letter to her son, David, that, following a strictly moderated diet over a sustained period, she had lost a fair bit of weight, reducing to 10.5 stones, which level she had maintained for over a year since. As a result of this, she said, and of changing her doctor, she felt she had renewed her youth. *'I never felt better in my life'*, she wrote. *'I can now run about like a young thing!'* When out feeding the hens she admitted to being surprised by her own agility. *'I can just pick up my two buckets and tear along as fast as anyone'*!

Indeed, so full of vitality did she feel that in the summer of the same year that I went to Balmacara, my mother also made a rare trip south, with the purpose of paying visits to her offspring who had moved to live on the mainland. It proved to be to all of them a most welcome visit, not least because of how events were soon to sadly pan out.

Back home at *Innister*, my mother kept up contact with family members outwith Rousay in the form of letter writing, as she had always been so faithful in doing. Corresponding with Sydney in Wick in November 1948, she doted over all her various grandchildren, several of whom she had seen, held, and cuddled for the first time on her summer visit south. In her epistle – for my mother wrote long letters - she detailed the features of each child, noting their age, and remarking on which close relative they resembled, etc., as any proud grandmother would be prone to do.

As the letter proceeded, my mother turned to those more advanced in age, lamenting the unusually high number of sudden deaths in Rousay in recent weeks - from a variety of causes - and including one or two in Wasbister itself. Somewhat ironically, within just a week or two of noting these local bereavements, my mother became ill herself and was confined to bed, heart-problems again returning to haunt her. Following a short period of illness, she passed away early the following year, on the 13th January, 1949, aged sixty-six. She was buried in Wasbister cemetery, alongside her beloved husband.

- - - - - - - - - - - - - -

Reflection

I secured a couple of maid-servant jobs in both Kirkwall and Orphir in those early years after leaving Rousay, before obtaining work as cook at the *Balfour Hospital* in 1950. I worked there for five years, cooking for up to ninety people, including nurses and domestic staff. I loved my time there, and retain memories of a whole further series of unique stories from this era – one of the happiest periods of my life. Certainly I had to work really hard, and it was a most responsible job. But I loved it all the same, and made a great many friends, both within the hospital – nurses as well as domestic staff – and without.

In 1956 I married Thomas Turfus Harvey Lennie (Tommy to all who knew him; his full name, like my own, being quite a mouthful!). Tommy was a young building contractor and stone mason from Orphir. Thus began a whole new chapter in my life. We settled down in the mainland parish of my husband's birth, living in a house built largely by himself. Here we raised a family of four – Maureen, Lorraine, Tommy and Audrey. Tragically, our precious Lorraine died of leukaemia in 1964, aged just four, a deeply traumatic experience for both her parents. My husband devoted himself to his work, and was considered by many a master of his craft. He also had a very social nature, and was well-liked in the community. I resided in Orphir for over half a century – fifty-seven years in all, and I suppose that if I wanted, a whole other book could be written on events of those years.

In 2012, following the death of my husband after some years battling with dementia, I moved to Kirkwall. Here I am happily settled, and am afforded the time to reminisce on my childhood years – a childhood so vastly different in every way from those of my own children and more so of my grandchildren and great-grandchildren. It was a childhood full of much joy and laughter, as well as, at times,

deep hurts and sorrows. A childhood that involved enormously hard work but also afforded wonderful occasions of immense enjoyment. An eventful childhood, graced by a multitude of colourful characters – some of whom became life-long friends. Most of these dear friends – including all my brothers and sisters except my younger sister – have since passed on. Why I have been granted the grace to remain so long, I cannot tell. But remaining with me to this day are countless memories of days gone by. Memories of events that time has as yet been unable to erase. Of course with my age increasing, my memory isn't nearly as sharp as it used to be. But I'm so fortunate to say that for all these long years and up to the present day, I've been able to mind these childhood stories as weel as can be.